D1052949

A Preface to American Political Theory

American Political Thought
edited by
Wilson Carey McWilliams and Lance Banning

A Preface
to American
Political Theory

Donald S. Lutz

JA 84 .U5 L88 1992
Lutz, Donald S.
A preface to American
    political theory

University Press of Kansas

Community College of Southern Nevada
Learning Resources Center
West Charleston Campus

APR 1 2 1995

© 1992 by the University Press of Kansas
All rights reserved

Published by the University Press of Kansas (Lawrence, Kansas 66049), which was
organized by the Kansas Board of Regents and is operated and funded by Emporia State
University, Fort Hays State University, Kansas State University, Pittsburg State University,
the University of Kansas, and Wichita State University

Library of Congress Cataloging-in-Publication Data

Lutz, Donald S.
    A preface to American political theory / Donald S. Lutz.
        p.   cm. — (American political thought)
    Includes bibliographical references and index.
    ISBN 0-7006-0545-2 (alk. paper)—ISBN 0-7006-0546-0 (pbk. : alk. paper)
    1. Political science—United States. I. Title. II. Series.
JA84.U5L88 1992
320.5'0973—dc20   92-11700

British Library Cataloguing in Publication Data is available.

Printed in the United States of America
10 9 8 7 6 5 4 3 2 1

The paper used in this publication meets the minimum requirements of the American
National Standard for Permanence of Paper for Printed Library Materials Z39.48-1984.

For Linda and Austin

Contents

Tables

Introduction

What follows is a book aimed at the student or researcher who is about to begin disciplined study of American political theory. Considerable emphasis is placed on clarifying the core of that discipline and its attendant methodologies, so that it will be clearly distinguishable from other intellectual enterprises. Such clarification is essential if we are to emancipate American political theorists from dominance by either an antitheoretical empiricism or by European methodologies and theories that are inappropriate to the American context. Such emancipation requires a more distinct and coherent identity for American political theory than it has now, but the task of clarifying its identity is complicated because that identity includes parts of those very approaches from which it is to be distinguished. For example, American political theory must be distinguished from narrow empiricism, yet systematic empirical study is an essential part of American political theory. Indeed, the very essence of American political theory, that which identifies its core and differentiates it from other branches of study, is the insistence on yoking together intellectual traditions and modes of study—normative, empirical, and analytic—that have tended to drift apart into camps characterized by either antagonism or mutual indifference.

If successful, what follows will help rescue American political theory from the undeserved status of a very subordinate subfield of political theory. This subordination results from the tendency of people in other areas of inquiry to claim the entire enterprise as their own and either to apply narrow criteria from their respective approaches, against which American political theory fails to measure up, or to use methodologies that intrude upon a balanced study and skew the results. American political theory from these various points of view is theoretically derivative, nonphilosophical, merely ideological, or empirically incoherent. That is, the tendency of scholars to treat American political theory in an offhanded manner largely reaffirms the status of the field as an intellectual backwater. The solution is to create a standard of scholarship against which these intrusions will be seen for what they are. Such a standard of scholarship requires us to define a body of material to be mastered, to learn a set of relevant methodologies and their proper usage, and to think through more carefully the mental stance the material and its study require us to adopt. In sum, this book is an introduction to the mental discipline required of students of American political theory who will set the standards for inquiry in the future.

Chapter 1

What Is American Political Theory?

The Status of the Discipline

American political theory, as a discipline, is waiting to be born. Its various pieces are floating free of each other in different academic departments and among several subfields within political science. What, one might ask, can those scholars who study political philosophy, voting behavior, legal history, philosophy, social history, legislative roll calls, public law, the history of ideas, economic theory, political sociology, and American literature have in common? One answer is that people from each of these intellectual pursuits have made and continue to make contributions to American political theory. The problem does not lie in the diversity of backgrounds but in an unsystematic focus, in the failure to ask what we are doing when we engage in the study of a subject called American political theory.

A kind of quiet modus vivendi has resulted from a common target of inquiry—the American founding. The importance of this event in human history and for the American experience has made the founding era a magnet for American academics of every description, and the common focus has served as an anchor. Yet the moment we seek the roots of this founding or ask how the founding relates to political thinking and activities that come later, conflicting assumptions and methodologies drive apart the various pieces that make up American political theory. Furthermore, this modus vivendi has led to the tendency to assume that nothing of consequence for American political theory came before the founding era and that nothing of much consequence happened afterward. The nineteenth century in America is generally ignored as a wasteland of political theory, and political theory in the twentieth century, including current approaches, is usually seen as unconnected to the issues of the founding era.

The creation of a discipline called American political theory does not require that we break off from other approaches to the study of politics. Instead, I argue that the discipline of our enterprise must assume the ability systematically to learn, use, and sometimes merge the approaches of these various other viewpoints. This in turn requires that we think more carefully about what it is we are doing when we engage in American political theory, that we become more self-conscious about our aims, assumptions, and methods.

A discipline necessarily implies a certain level of intellectual rigor, a set of important and difficult questions that serve as the focus of inquiry, and a methodology appropriate to the study of these questions that is both effective and sophisticated. Such an activity requires that those scholars engaged in it should have undergone an intellectual formation, a disciplining of the mind, that prepared them. A discipline, in other words, is a joint enterprise engaged in by a number of people who have undergone a certain intellectual formation so that they understand the common questions defining the enterprise, have a comprehensive familiarity with the relevant literature and materials, and know how to use the methodologies appropriate for advancing that literature.

"Discipline" is not used here in the loose academic sense to identify heterogeneous conglomerates of scholars gathered in a specific university department, such as the "discipline" of political science. Political science is currently more of an academic profession composed of several disciplines linked by a modus vivendi. There is, for example, a discipline within the profession built around the close textual analysis of a well-defined canon of great books, which requires both the mastery of the contents of these works and the techniques of textual analysis with which to study them. Another discipline requires mastery of a literature based upon the empirical study of political phenomena as well as upon the statistical, inferential, and research-design techniques required to evaluate and extend such research. We can identify other disciplines within political science, such as those built around formal mathematics or around a foreign language, but the main point to be grasped here is that within the profession of political science there are several disciplines, each requiring that the person practicing it be formed and developed in a certain way.

A "discipline" is defined by a specific, rigorous intellectual formation; a "profession" is a body of persons that has licensed or publicly certified that its members have attained a certain minimal level of proficiency in the delivery of a service. Presumably, since a profession is usually deemed to require some form of advanced training, one must successfully undergo a discipline in order to be licensed as a professional. Therefore a discipline refers to a process that is open in the sense that it never ends, either in its development or in its application, and anyone can decide to enter it, even amateurs; a profession refers to a status that is by definition closed—both in the sense that the status is closed to those who have not been licensed and in the sense that once the status is attained, no further development is required to retain the status.

The current idea of a professional contains two interesting ambiguities. First, we speak of someone who engages in a specific activity for a livelihood as a professional (a professional writer, for example), but at the same time the essence of a profession is that "though men enter it for the sake of a livelihood, the measure of their success is the service they perform not the gains which they amass."[1] In other words, professionals do not "keep score" by the amount of money they make but by some professional standard, such as the number and quality of their publications, discoveries, patents, cures, or successful court cases and the recognition given these "scores" through various forms of nonmonetary awards and honors. A second ambiguity relates to the need for a professional to "profess" something as true—in the old days one professed a faith—and at the same time to follow inherent professional standards of neutrality and universal applicability. Essentially a professional professes a high level of standards in the delivery of a service, but he or she also professes that a certain discipline will be most likely to produce that high level of service. For this reason a profession requires a licensing system, both to ensure standards and to keep out those who have not undergone a proper discipline.

Every profession, although it licenses for a common, minimal discipline, still contains within itself a variety of disciplines that have developed above and beyond that common discipline. For example, medicine requires a common American Medical Association license as a minimum before a person can be called "doctor," but the discipline of a surgeon is not the same as that of a pediatrician, a psychiatrist, or an ophthalmologist, each of which requires substantial training beyond medical school. Of course, each branch of medicine has its more advanced and specialized certification, but pediatrics is a specialty and medicine is the profession. In the same way political science is a profession that defines a minimum, common certification but that contains a number of specialties defined by a more advanced discipline. Unlike medical schools, however, where each specialty is organized in a separate department, political science combines its various disciplines in a single department.

On the one hand, the presence of several disciplines within a single university department tends to divide those scholars who are ultimately studying the same subject or set of phenomena. This diversity has required over the past century an almost continuous accommodation among disciplines within political science departments, an accommodation that has often been acrimonious since the wedge that divides the parties is much more than methodological diversity. On the other hand, the presence of several disciplines in the same department has had the beneficial effect of continuously reinforcing in everyone's mind those features that the various parties do share—a common interest in the study of politics and a common dedication to the highest level of disciplined inquiry. The competition and the mutual opposition have led proponents of each discipline to shore up and improve their respective positions, not to the point where the uneasy accommodation is based upon mutual agreement, but to the extent that each advocate at least recognizes that the others do impose a training, an orderly and difficult set of standards, upon themselves and their students, which constitutes disciplined political inquiry. They sometimes see in each other patterns of inquiry that are misguided and fruitless, but the accommodation tends to be based upon a quiet acknowledgment that the others do pursue a recognizable discipline of the mind.

To a certain extent this recognition is manifested through the publication of scholarly books and articles. No matter how little regard one discipline might receive and despite some striking differences in opinion over the preferred publication pattern, three characteristics together create the operational definition of a successful political scientist: (1) a systematic inquiry more or less guided by rigorous methodology, (2) the development from that inquiry of a sustained analysis and argument that proceeds according to recognizable canons of logic, and (3) success in passing a refereed evaluation by a group of one's peers to produce a publication in a respected forum. Put another way, the tendency in political science is to define a discipline as the combination of systematic inquiry, logical exposition, and successful "marketplace" (i.e., neutral) evaluation—with all three combining to discipline the work of an individual.

This publication-based modus vivendi among the various disciplines within political science has had some generally beneficial effects beyond reinforcing a recognition of shared interests and dedication. A primary benefit has been an advance in sophistication by almost all of the disciplines in the profession as a result of the stimulation produced by deep, mutual critiques. Another has been the tendency to continue the exposure of doctoral students in their formal training to several political science disciplines (except in those relatively rare and unfortunate instances where one discipline or another has "captured" a department), which has the result of internalizing the disciplinary tensions within individuals in a way that often produces a useful self-critique, quiet though it may be.

In the context of this divided yet accommodated profession called political science, American political theory has an unusual place that is presently anomalous but potentially important. American political theory is not yet a discipline since those who say they are engaged in the enterprise offer several competing versions, none of which is adequate as a discipline because each is partial—partial in the double sense of being incomplete in its definition of the project and of favoring or being biased toward one of the other relevant disciplines in political science. This partiality is a result of the history of political science in America.

Born as an American profession in the late nineteenth and early twentieth century (although the systematic study of politics was born twenty-five hundred years ago in Greece), political science was at first heavily oriented toward the theoretical discussion of American politics and political institutions.[2] One could almost say that the field we currently tend to call American political theory was in the beginning the core of American academic discourse about politics. As the profession was gradually fragmented into specializations, pieces of the total enterprise pulled away from this core and developed distinct identities within the profession, often defined by their own methodologies as well as by more narrowly focused research. As a result, over the years American political theory has become almost a residual category, that which remains after everyone else has left.

The peculiar position of American political theory within political science can be illustrated in several ways. The American Political Science Association publishes a yearly membership directory that lists its approximately ten thousand members in a variety of ways, including by specialty. The association recognizes twenty-six fields of interest, but American political theory is not one of them.[3] Still, virtually every political science department has someone teaching American political theory, sometimes more than one person, and American political theory is usually part of the standard introductory American government course. Yet the job listings almost never have ads recruiting scholars in American political theory. Instead, there is usually a sentence that lists American political theory as one of several possibilities for ancillary interest in addition to the area or specialty for which the person will be hired.[4] As a result, those teaching American political theory tend to come to it through the back door and lack a common disciplinary base.

Once, at a conference attended by nineteen well-published scholars in American political theory, I asked the participants what subjects they had been originally hired to teach. The responses included: American political theory (two), history of political thought (two), public policy, political behavior, international relations, medieval political thought, methodology, constitutional law, voting behavior, the presidency and congress, urban politics, public administration, public law, statistics, modern political theory, state politics, and public choice. Although this sample was hardly random, the phenomenon of teachers of American political theory coming to the task from another part of the profession is familiar enough to those of us involved that the sample is recognizable as reasonably representative.

Nor is this necessarily an unhealthy phenomenon; there is much to be said for making American political theory the meeting place of the discipline. Furthermore, the nature of American political theory is such that as an enterprise it must draw upon and relate to many or most of the specializations that have withdrawn from it. Earlier reference was made to the critical potential of American political theory, and this potential lies in using its natural connectedness to the various disciplines within political science to aid the development of a comprehensive, coherent study of political phenomena that moves beyond the current minimally accommodating, mutually suspicious, haphazardly reinforcing divided activity.

One major purpose of this book is to offer a vision of a discipline called American political theory and its requirements from its practitioners in terms of common preparation. The book is in this sense a preface to a discipline, an invitation to an explicit, orderly discussion about what those of us who teach, think about, and write in American political theory are doing and should do. The intent, however, is not to erect fences within political science, to create an orthodoxy, or to develop criteria for licensing practitioners in American political theory. Rather, anyone who is interested in pursuing the study of American political theory, those scholars in another discipline (in the sense of a departmentalized profession such as history or philosophy), other academics elsewhere in political science, or anyone outside of the academy—whether they are students by matriculation, amateur interest, or cross-disciplinary research—all are invited to view this book as an aid to study, as an introduction to the topic, as a preface to a discipline struggling to be born.

What is American Political *Theory*?

The first step in our analysis is to reach a provisional understanding of the three terms that define the enterprise—American, political, and theory. Each term has multiple usages and meanings that are confused and confounded, and therefore we must draw some important distinctions. My strategy here is to lay out the major alternative understandings of each term and then to suggest which of these apply most appropriately to the pursuit of American political theory. The discussion is designed to be useful and evocative rather than to resolve the ambiguity and contradictions. If the discussion is successful, those readers who disagree with my position will know precisely where the disagreement lies.

The term "theory" has in various contexts been used interchangeably with a number of other terms such as "philosophy," "thought," "ideology," and "hypothesis." For example, in everyday, ordinary language we often use the term in reference to a single statement that is contingent or hypothetical in nature. The classical formulation "If A, then B" is frequently termed a theory. Certainly a hypothesis is a theoretical statement, but a theory worthy of the name comprises a number of logically linked statements, not just one proposition. Implicit in such usage is the assumption that a theory is something not yet proven or for which there is not yet strong evidence. Perhaps this assumption results from the appropriation of the term from the physical sciences, where any statement, even if supported by evidence, is still considered falsifiable and therefore contingent rather than demonstrably true. Yet even in science, where all statements are to some extent contingent, "theory" is usually used in reference to a logically linked set of propositions that has significant empirical support. That is, a theory is both far more complex than a hypothesis because it is composed of many statements and less contingent than a hypothesis because its propositions are former hypotheses that have been to a greater or lesser extent supported by systematically gathered evidence. For these two reasons it is improper to use "theory" as equivalent to "hypothesis"; one cannot speak sensibly of "American political hypotheses" as an enterprise.

One can speak of "American political thought," however, and this is the phrase most commonly used in the titles of books that supposedly introduce the subject. Certainly theoretical thinking is the attempt to be thoughtful in the sense of seeking to be serious in purpose, careful in reasoning, and cautious in reaching conclusions; moreover, "thought" does refer to the process of conceiving ideas and of reflecting upon them or to the ideas that result from reasoning. But theory is not the same thing as thought. Thought encompasses the processes and results of spiritual meditation, imaginative and creative invention, stream-of-consciousness randomness, conditioned cognitive responses, opinions based upon prejudice, and untested or untestable common-sense propositions. Theory, on the other hand, implies a careful, considered, logically structured explanation for an event or events that is susceptible to modification or rejection on the basis of further systematically presented information—either through empirical research (science) or through the rigorous explication of implications (philosophy).

An examination of the prominent textbooks with American political *thought* in the title shows that they typically contain either partial texts by a large number of people expressing a wide range of opinion or that they discuss a wide range of thinkers in some kind of historical context.[5] In the case of edited collections, because the arguments are usually just a part of a person's position, a complete theory cannot be laid out. Not even the tenth essay of *The Federalist* constitutes a reasonably complete theory. Thus, political thoughts are presented that can encompass anything in the way of thought just outlined. In the case of the history of ideas, the tendency is to sacrifice the explication and discussion of theory and to replace it with summaries of the changes in dominant patterns of political thought. Such an approach also usually attempts to explain the factors that caused the changes in the patterns of thought shared by Americans at a given time.

A more careful examination of such books shows that they do not claim to present political theory but to represent or describe the ideas, principles, and opinions prevalent at a given time, among a given people, in a given place. In short, these books offer purportedly representative thoughts of certain groups or certain eras of American history or both. Such representations can be significant and are useful in a basic descriptive sense, but they do not constitute theory. The editors of such volumes, in the selection of their titles, tend to be very straightforward and honest about their goal, but the implications of such an introduction to American political theory are not helpful.

First, to use a book on political thought as an introduction to American political theory implies either that there is no difference between theory and thought or that there is no such thing as political theory. Second, such a presentation implies that the thoughts of all those writers in the book somehow have equal or equivalent theoretical status. Third, by implication theoretical importance is reduced to or confounded with its impact on the popular thought of an era, thus suggesting that ideas in general are rooted in and relevant only to particular historical circumstances. Let us consider each implication briefly in turn.

If no difference exists between theory and thought, then on what grounds are we to urge our students to seek deeper levels of understanding and more rigorous logical explanations? If teachers using such books do not point out the superior reasoning in one piece compared with another, regardless of the position being defended, then we might just as well let students go home, utter anything they wish, and mail them a degree. If there is no theory, then not only can there be no philosophical discourse about politics, there can be no science of politics either.

Nor is it helpful to suggest to students that all political thoughts have equivalent theoretical status. It is one thing for teachers to be patient with students who in their attempts at learning utter the silly or the banal; it is another thing to hold up to these students as a model of political discourse an amorphous melange that mixes the good with the bad and the ugly. Theory is built around an exploration of deeper, more fundamantal issues, and mixing theory with superficial political expostulations will understandably lead a student to conclude that the political correctness of a thought is more important than the reasoning that led to it.

The view that all thoughts on politics are equivalent in value is related to the confusion caused by confounding the importance of a theory with its impact on a given historical period. Any theory worthy of the name is a claim for some truth that transcends not only its historical era but also its culture and the intent of its discoverer. Good theory can be used by people of different ideologies, from different nations, and for opposing interests. For example, empirical theories about the impact of different electoral systems on party systems or the relative merits of congressional and parliamentary modes of organizing the legislature can be used by people on any continent in any year. Likewise, theories linking political institutions with preferred political outcomes can transcend the historical era and its place of origin. For an interesting example, one could compare John C. Calhoun's theory of the concurrent majority from the 1840s with the theory of black power enunciated in the

1960s. A striking similarity exists between a theory devised in support of slavery in the American south and a much later theory devised to advance the control of African Americans over their destiny. The point here is not to claim that Stokely Carmichael got his idea for black power from Calhoun; rather, it is to argue that Calhoun's theory could be used by others of a completely different persuasion because this transcendence is vital to good theory. It is one thing to ask about the historical impact of an idea or a theory at a particular time at a particular place and an entirely different thing to ask for the meaning and implications of a theory that is not necessarily bounded by time, place, or interest.

Failure to distinguish the meaning of a theory from its immediate historical impact is partly responsible for the tendency—now common among historians and political scientists—to confuse theory with ideology.[6] This confusion is based upon two premises: first, that all human ideas are conditioned by some aspect of the human environment, and second, that ideological thinking differs from nonideological thinking primarily by being more coherent in its logical structuring.

In its broad form the first premise holds that ideas do not have an independent existence but are reflections of processes and events in the material world. In its narrow form it holds that political theories are only ideas devised to protect, advance, and justify specific political interests at a particular time in history. For now it is sufficient to suggest that even if all political thinking is initially at the service of historical interests (a highly debatable presumption), political theory refers to political thinking that has a content and structure that allows it to be used by different, even opposing, interests at different points in history. If there is such a phenomenon, then political theory describes it, and a theory is distinguishable from an ideology—with the latter term reserved to describe the phenomenon of political thinking that is only in the service of a particular interest at a particular time.

This notion of particularity, of course, is the minimal basis for distinction. One might want to argue for a more definite distinction on the grounds that even though much or most political thinking is in the service of particular historical interests, some of this thinking may be of such a content and a structure that it can be used in a variety of historical settings by people with a variety of interests. Furthermore, it is perfectly possible that some political thinking can be devised that neither originates from narrow political interests nor is used directly in support of specific political interests. Put another way, political theory of some types may be so inherently opposed to supporting specific interests that it cannot be used for historically conditioned purposes. For now we will simply leave open this possibility, if for no other reason than that its status is one of the fundamental problems addressed by American political theory.

The second premise underlying the confusion between theory and ideology is descriptively correct but is often the basis for a faulty deduction. Ideologies do in fact have a logical structure that is similar to and often indistinguishable from that of theory. Political scientists speak of ideologies as being belief systems whose propositions are constrained or linked by an often elaborate logic. For example, in the study of voting behavior those voters who can give an explanation for their vote in terms of a set of propositions that are structured by a coherent, recognizable logic are termed "ideological voters."[7] These ideologies are recognizable to most students as "isms," such as liberalism, conservativism, communism, and so forth. Since these ideologies have internal structures the same as or similar to theories and since these ideologies usually can be attributed in origin to some well-known political theorist such as John Locke, Edmund Burke, or Karl Marx, the straightforward deduction emerges that ideologies are theories, and thus theories must be ideologies.

Undoubtedly theories can be used as ideologies, but are theories automatically ideologies? The confusion results from comparing the internal structures of theories and ideologies instead of considering the purpose and the psychological status of each. Another line of study has determined that one key attribute of an ideology is the tendency of its holder to use it for psychological protection.[8] That is, ideologies are elaborate rationalizations that help protect the individual's ego by helping that person deal with a complicated, changing world, by assisting in the creation and maintenance of a self-image, and by aiding in the processing of new, unfamiliar information. In short, ideologies are simply a more elaborate form of rationalization arising not from the need to protect one's objective interests but from psychological needs not necessarily tied to one's objective interests. Ideologies, from this point of view, arise from irrational needs.

This contrasting view of ideology serves to drive another wedge between ideology and theory. On the one hand, ideology is seen as the rational inclination to protect one's material interests; on the other hand, ideologies are viewed as serving one's irrational psychological needs, even at the expense of material interests. In this second view ideologies are used to filter out information that conflicts with the already existing view of the world, the self, and the place of the self in the world. Once formed, ideologies are resistant to change since the ego is so heavily invested in the existing belief system. This strong tendency for ideology to be resistant to factual information or to reasoned argument or to both really defines the phenomenon. Political theory provides a logical explanation for political events and processes that is by definition susceptible to change or to rejection on the basis of facts or arguments or both; ideology is a theory or theory-like belief system (that is, a structured argument) that is used for psychological protection such that it is resistant to alteration by facts or by reasoned argument.

Political theories may be used as ideologies, but they are not automatically ideologies. Part of the problem for theory that arises from the behavioral literature of political science results from the quite proper conclusion by behaviorists that since natural science proceeds on the basis of observables and since we can observe behavior but not motives, we cannot attribute a motive to an individual with any degree of scientific certainty. Thus we cannot behaviorally distinguish a structured argument that is being used to justify a material interest from one being used to defend the ego or distinguish either of these from one being used to seek truth. A problem arises from using the term ideology to describe voters with apparent theories: It simultaneously attributes them with two contradictory views of ideology, rational interest-seeking versus irrational ego protection, but leaves no room for truth-seeking. Unless the possibility of truth-seeking, and thus of theory, is allowed, however, one must attribute the same ideological purpose to behavioral research, in which case the work of empirical political science must either be viewed as in the service of some material interest of the behaviorists or else be seen as serving to satisfy some irrational need of the researcher.

The relationship of theory to ideology is thus such that a theory can be used as an ideology, but theory and ideology are not the same since theory is in some sense always truth-seeking, something that by definition ideology cannot be (although an ideology could be correct or true by accident). A final, important distinction remains to be made between theory and philosophy, a distinction that raises some serious questions for American political theory as a discipline.

It is a matter of more than passing interest that one never reads or hears of American political *philosophy*. The phrase seems somehow pretentious or inappropriate, but the unwillingness to use it has serious implications. It is standard in the political science literature to look upon the activities of political philosophers as being essentially normative; their concern is with moral, ethical, or value judgments.[9] This view distinguishes political philosophy from the empirical tasks of describing and explaining political phenomena, termed political science. Since the most prominent American political theorists include men like James Madison, Thomas Jefferson, and John Adams—who were directly involved in some aspect of our nation's founding—any refusal to call them political philosophers implies that the founding of our political system did not involve normative considerations, that our political system was not designed to be "good," and also that no one since then has been concerned with the manner and extent to which our political system might be considered good. Obviously this is not true. Thus to the extent that American political thought has included concern for matters like virtue, the goodness or badness of public policy, and the justice or worth of our national political institutions and processes, American political theory is open to the possibility of concerning itself with political philosophy.

Some scholars would argue that although they are willing to include normative concerns under the term American political theory, the absence in American political thinking of architectonic political philosophies of the kind associated with Plato, Aristotle, Locke, Marx, or Mill justifies our not using American political philosophy as the description of our enterprise. This softened position is open to two criticisms, however. First, Plato, Aristotle, and other recognized philosophers did not argue that the creation of large, complicated theories was needed before the term "philosophy" could be applied to the effort. Instead, philosophy has always been viewed as a *process of seeking* the truth, not as the production of grandiose texts. Second, this position begs one of the critical questions that American political theory must consider—the extent to which American politics has been guided by normative concerns, the extent to which it should be so governed, and by what values. In sum, even if there are no identifiable individuals in American history with the philosophical stature of a Plato or an Aristotle, the possibility still obtains that this book should more properly be entitled *A Preface to American Political Philosophy*.

Political philosophy properly understood is not opposed to the empirical study of politics; instead, political philosophy includes political science. This can be illustrated by considering the various questions that a student of politics might ask. First, one might ask for a description of how current political institutions and processes work; a response would involve a descriptive task that falls under empirical political science. One could then ask how change in political institutions occurs, including how and why our current ones came into being. These are also empirical questions, but they require an explanatory rather than a descriptive response.

Humans engage in science primarily because they prefer to understand their situation rather than to remain ignorant. Furthermore, humans developed language, culture, social systems, and institutions for making collective decisions. Language allowed the creation of culture through which to pass knowledge from generation to generation. Culture, over time, permitted the creation of large, stable societies, which required institutions to maintain and to give them direction. This in turn required making choices, and politics was developed to replace choice imposed by force and violence with choice based upon persuasion.

The art of persuasion is known as rhetoric; political rhetoric aims at winning the arguments about which direction a society should take. In classical Greece rhetoric spawned a competitor that sought not merely to win the argument but to provide an understanding of which direction society should take. Political philosophy was based upon the search for the good political system. Rhetoric was intended to teach individuals how to be persuasive in support of their narrow interests, but political philosophy was intended to teach them how to be persuasive in support of broader, shared human ends. Indeed, the belief that all humans had vital ends that they shared was the ground from which political philosophy arose.

Political philosophy required that a distinction be made between people's real needs and what they thought they wanted without proper reflection. It also required that we understand the nature of politics, its institutions and processes, and the range of possibilities open to humans on an imperfect earth. Aristotle organized political questions in a way that can be illustrated by a continuum representing an infinite number of possible-states-of-affairs merging into one another and arranged by their relative closeness to an ideal.

Aristotle argues that first one must have a standard by which to evaluate the present, and it seems reasonable to use the best standard, the ideal. The first task, then, is to analyze the implication of the ideal and to determine why the ideal is worth pursuing. The former is an analytical undertaking; the latter is a normative one. The ideal defines the end of the continuum, but the nature of the human situation is such that it is not possible to have the ideal in the real world as opposed to the world of ideas. The question, then, is to ask how closely the ideal can be approached in the real world (represented by point A). The answer involves a prudential calculation based upon the best empirical information available and a clear understanding of the goals and ideals relevant to the decision. For example, if our ideal is justice, to approach it too closely might entail serious compromise with respect to the ideals of equality or stability. That is, since no one ideal, and thus no one continuum, can encompass all that is of value to humans, a highly developed sense of the normative must be brought to bear on the available information in order to answer this question.

Point B represents our place on the continuum at the moment. This determination must be made empirically, but note that without a normative context, the continuum to define the situation, this empirical question cannot be sensibly answered. Point C represents the point where we wish to go next, in part because it is closer to the ideal and in part because we wish to test what happens when we move closer to the ideal. Empirical political science has as one of its aims the ability to tell us how to adjust institutions in order to move from B to C, but the reasons that we might want to do so belong more properly in the realm that some call critical theory, which is a manifestation of normative theory.[10]

Thus, in Aristotle's conceptualization, empirical political science is a part of the total analysis encompassed by political philosophy, rather than being in opposition to it. Political theory cannot be isolated from political philosophy, since its three forms—empirical theory, analytic theory, and normative theory—are each subparts of the general philosophical program. Political philosophy can be called the enterprise that encompasses, indeed requires, all three forms of theory. Political theory can thus be used as a linguistic alternative to political philosophy, even though the latter is a whole and the former implies parts of the same whole.

The word "theory" in the book's title is intended not only to signal the possibility of there being an American political philosophy or philosophies but also to imply that the enterprise includes all three forms of theoretical discourse.

What Is American *Political* Theory?

American political theory as a discipline should be defined by the systematic, cumulative activities of scholars engaged in the common enterprise of studying American politics theoretically. Yet even this seemingly tautological description hides a serious ambiguity that prevents American political theory from becoming a true discipline. The ambiguity results from the widely noted lack of a definition for politics to use as a focus for the common enterprise.[11]

There has been a varied response to this lack of a common definition. Some scholars turn it into a virtue by arguing that any attempt to define politics is a waste of time and energy at best and is probably dangerous because it prematurely limits the scope of study.[12] Most scholars working in political science or American political theory probably accept this position or its variant, that because of continued definitional diversity the best we can do is to define political science as the field that political scientists study, and thus politics is whatever those who study it say it is.[13] Still, despite the general belief that a definition is dangerous or unnecessary, most scholars writing theoretically about politics feel compelled to associate themselves with some definition, perhaps in uneasy agreement with E.E. Schattschneider's caution that

> there is something strange about the feeling of scholars that a definition [of politics] is not necessary. Inevitably there is a lack of focus in the discipline because it is difficult to see things that are undefined. People who cannot define the object of their studies do not know what they are looking for, and if they do not know what they are looking for, how can they tell when they have found it?

Schattschneider then compares political science without a definition of politics to "a mountain of data surrounding a vacuum."[14]

Schattschneider is probably correct in his intuition that a definition is needed but too demanding in his expectations for that definition. Certainly any definition should permit us in general to distinguish the political from the nonpolitical, but it is not clear that the definition needs to be so precise that it allows no room for argument. Indeed, more explicit argument about the nature of politics should be allowed by any definition since such arguments are the essence of politics. With this in mind, we shall briefly examine a number of prominent definitions, develop a characterization of politics from them that quietly informs contemporary political science, and then show how American political theory has an implicit operational definition of politics that is both consistent with this characterization and less problematic in its provisions for distinguishing the political from the nonpolitical.

Let us begin by considering a number of characterizations that have been advanced by prominent students of politics.[15] The first is representative of a more traditional approach to the study of American politics that predominated before the mid-1950s. "The central point of attention in American political science . . . is that part of the affairs of the state which centers in government, and that kind or part of government which speaks through law" (Charles S. Hyneman).[16] Hyneman's characterization emphasizes the importance of laws and institutions to politics, although his first four words allow for much more to be included on the periphery of attention. Still, critics of such a view argue for a definition that allows more prominent inclusion of processes that are less formally, less directly part of governmental institutions. Initially such critics were especially interested in adding political parties, interest groups, and bureaucratic decision making to the central framework of American political theory; a decision-making approach seemed most useful toward this end.

"Politics or the political includes the events that happen around the decision-making centers of government" (Alfred de Grazia).[17] De Grazia's characterization retains the link between politics and governmental institutions but opens up the political to include events that might affect governmental decision making. Economic and social processes that impinge on decision making thus become fair game, or fairer game since it is not clear that Hyneman's definition excludes such considerations beyond denying their centrality for study. A decision-making approach has a number of other virtues, not the least of which is its more explicit introduction of the study of conflict and cooperation into political analysis. In sum, a decision-making definition of politics is broader and more inclusive than a definition that emphasizes governmental institutions and introduces more explicitly the notions of social process, conflict, and cooperation into the study of politics.

For a long while, however, some scholars had been concerned that a definition that limited politics to the governmental was unduly narrow for political scientists who wanted to study a broader range of phenomena. For example, it was argued, political scientists might encounter tribal societies that lacked formal governmental institutions, but they should be free to study such societies. In retrospect this example offered a strange basis upon which to argue for a definition of politics that denied the centrality of governmental institutions for politics. By the time political science became a profession in the twentieth century the number of people living in a tribal condition was extremely small and rapidly disappearing. Political scientists tend to have cognate fields of study toward which their research opens, whether it be history, sociology, philosophy, psychology, or anthropology, and sometimes political scientists will find a need to enter this cognate field completely in their research. Why could not those studying tribal societies admit that they were in effect anthropologists studying prepolitical phenomena? Their insistence upon a definition of politics that included a form of social organization that once had been profoundly important and interesting but that now had become largely ephemeral did not advance the study of tribal forms very much; instead it led to a view of politics that could no longer be used to distinguish the political from the nonpolitical. Whatever the extent to which the anthropological view rested upon the study of tribal society, the virtual disappearance of pure tribal organization into settings conditioned by governmental institutions has rendered this anthropological need for a noninstitutional definition of politics, indeed the entire approach, moribund.

A more lasting and coherent position in favor of a broad definition of politics views human behavior as constituting a seamless web that can be analyzed in all its parts, using relatively few concepts. Since political scientists are greatly interested in power, some have argued that power is the essence of the political.

"The political process is the shaping, distribution, and exercise of power. . . . Political science is concerned with power in general" (Harold Lasswell and Abraham Kaplan).[18] Lasswell and Kaplan's definition is intuitively appealing, and it really is difficult to think of a political decision, process, or situation that does not involve power. Yet it is possible to think of many situations involving power that are not political. Throwing a shot-put involves power, but if throwing the put is also political then we have lost all ability to distinguish the political from the nonpolitical, and we no longer have a useful, functioning definition. The example, some readers will say, is unfair since it confuses physical power with political power, but Lasswell and Kaplan's definition does not make such a distinction. Nor does their definition distinguish between being robbed at gunpoint and serving on a jury or between the use of military force and the Supreme Court's applying the U.S. Bill of Rights against the states. All are included as political phenomena so that it is now perfectly sensible to speak of the "politics of the family." Some political scientists may be happy with a definition that supports acts of professional imperialism whenever it strikes our fancy, but the word "politics" is inherited from Greek origins that made such distinctions precisely because politics was the replacement of force with persuasion and because politics involved the marriage or blending of justice with power. The definition of politics as simply power, then, is analytically useless since it cannot distinguish the political from the nonpolitical, linguistically barbarous since it empties an old term of its normal meaning, and empirically problematic since we are unable to apply the term without solving the analytic and linguistic problems.

Perhaps for these reasons, except for a general agreement that politics always includes power, today relatively few political scientists equate politics with power. William Bluhm's definition of politics is interesting since it includes power as part of a broader decision-making approach: "Reduced to its universal elements, then, politics is a social process characterized by activity involving rivalry and cooperation in the exercise of power, and culminating in the making of decisions for a group."[19]

Although Lasswell and Kaplan's definition is not used much anymore, David Easton's definition is widely accepted and used by political scientists: "Political life consists of those actions related to the authoritative allocation of values for a society."[20] The term "values" refers to anything upon which humans place a value, whether material, spiritual, or symbolic, and thus the definition looks at first like an inclusive one; however, the key operative word would appear to be "authoritative." If power refers to the ability of A to get B to do something B would otherwise not do, authority refers to the exercise of power by A that is viewed by B as legitimate.[21] Thus, a robber does not legitimately take my money, but under properly political conditions the tax man legitimately does so. It is difficult to see how authority can exist apart from governmental institutions if one is allocating values in such a way that the allocation is viewed as legitimate by an entire society, and thus Easton's definition does not really differ much from Hyneman's in its breadth or in its implications.

In any case, the easy affinity between Hyneman's and Easton's definitions is illustrated in other definitions generated by political scientists in an attempt to understand the object of their study. Alan C. Isaak offers a good example: "Politics has something to do with the use of power to reconcile conflicts over the distribution of goods and values. Typically, this is done through the institutions of government."[22] Note that most of the language from the decision-making approach is also present in Isaak's definition, although the use of "distribution" here, just as the use of "alloca-tion" in Easton's definition, has some troubling implications. Primarily, the implication is that politics somehow works from the top down, going from the authorities to those below them; in contrast, a pure decision-making language implies that a group of people in a horizontal relationship can reach a collective decision on their own without reference to a hierarchy. Also, many decisions, such as electing people to office, amending a constitution, and deciding whether a person is guilty of a crime, are made by an electorate or a jury and are not distributions or allocations of values as much as they are the defining of, the exercising of, and the imposing of values from below. Since much of politics in America depends upon these "values from below," a definition of politics useful for American political theory might be better served by decision-making language.

Also missing from these definitions are the two notions that politics is at minimum the substitution of persuasion for force and that in its complete sense politics is the process of seeking the good life, or *eudaemonia*. Theorists such as Christian Bay update this second notion of Aristotle's by arguing that politics involves the building of a just community based upon fundamental human needs that are both material and spiritual.[23]

One can see in Isaak the straining toward a definition that on the one hand includes everything that needs to be included and on the other excludes what needs to be excluded. Politics has "something to do" with power and conflict, and "typically" governmental institutions are involved. That most recent definitions of politics contain such strained construction does not reflect the lack of consensus among political scientists about the constitution of politics; rather, it reflects the difficulty of precisely defining anything so amorphous. Nor does the difficulty suggest that we should do without a definition, since, for example, research on American politics does not require a definition that can cover tribal society. Indeed, any useful definition in the American context will describe politics as we practice it.

David W. Minar correctly notes that the American political system is above all constitutional, which explains why so many books on American political theory contain "constitution" in their titles and why American political theory seems naturally to gravitate toward an analysis that includes discussion of the founding era. Though Minar's definition is not entirely felicitous, it points us in an interesting direction: "By politics we mean a process for the seeking of authoritative solutions to social problems, by constitution, a generalized guide to this process."[24]

The cramped prose reflects an attempt to include the basics of Easton's definition, a sign of its hold on mainstream political science. Yet if we consider Easton's phrase "authoritative allocation of value" and ask what aspect of American politics makes anything authoritative, the answer has to be popular consent as embodied in a constitution.

American political theory has always worked implicitly from an operational definition of politics based on constitutionalism; that is, politics consists of processes conditioned by a written constitution. In other words, in order for something to be considered political, it must be brought under the description of the constitution. Obviously this means that institutions described in the constitution are political, but so are processes that are related to the operation of those institutions. Thus, political parties are political because they operate in the context of elections, and elections are constitutionally conditioned. Without the constitution, there would be no elections and thus no parties. Interest groups operate in the context of elections or of the branches of government created by the constitution. Bureaucratic processes are political if the bureaucracy belongs to an executive branch created by a constitution and charged with the task of carrying out legislation passed by another constitutional creation—the legislature.

Our federal structure creates national, state, and local constitutions so that we have politics in all of these arenas. Until and unless an issue is brought under the constitutional umbrella, until it is brought into the public realm, it remains in the private or nonpolitical realm. Congress can appropriate an issue to the public, constitutional realm by passing legislation affecting that activity, or it can move the issue back into the private sphere. In the same way the Supreme Court can interpret the Constitution so as to include or remove an issue from the political realm. Much constitutional controversy, including matters of rights, occurs in debate over whether issues should be defined as political rather than as private.

The use of constitutionalism to define politics in America is also an efficient and effective way of including issues that most political scientists wish to include as political phenomena while at the same time denoting the nonpolitical with reasonable clarity. In another context I laid out the purposes for which Americans write constitutions; in this context these purposes serve to define the core of the political for American political theory.[25] Any American constitution worthy of the name will

1. Define a way of life—the values, major principles, and definition of justice toward which a people aim
2. Create and/or define the people of the community so directed
3. Define the political institutions, the process of collective decision making, to be instrumental in achieving the way of life—in other words, define a form of government
4. Define the regime, the public, and citizenship
5. Establish the basis for the authority of the regime
6. Distribute political power
7. Structure conflict so it can be managed
8. Limit governmental power.

Here we have a summary of the meaning of politics. Matters that most political scientists want to include are here included—if not explicitly, then by direct implication. Any behavior relevant to the definition of politics contained in a constitution is political behavior. Questions of philosophy or of theory relevant to this definition of politics are part of political philosophy or political theory. State and urban politics, intergovernmental relations, presidential and legislative studies, parties and pressure groups, elections and public opinion, constitutional law and judicial process, public policy and public administration—everything now considered part of the study of American politics is included. The definition is also flexible because constitutions can be amended or replaced to include new institutions, include different values, redistribute political power, or alter the understanding of citizenship so that, for example, matters of race, gender, ethnicity, morals, or economics that were not before considered part of politics become political and thus part of the material that political scientists study.

Ultimately, the empirical study of politics boils down to the search for patterns or regularities in human behavior. We conduct such a search because we wish to understand the grounding for such behavior but also because we hope to use our understanding of these patterns and regularities for prediction. In political science prediction proceeds at several levels. At the most superficial level we wish to predict the outcome of specific historical events, such as elections, legislative roll calls, or judicial decisions, to name just a few examples. As social scientists we have deeper, more important goals, however—predicting across several events to define the probable consequences of a policy and predicting across an even wider range of events to define the probable operation and consequences of institutions and political processes. This last level is that of constitutionalism and constitutional design.

As we move from more specific to more general problems of prediction, a sound political science is likely to be more helpful because it is not necessary that prediction go beyond the most general, statistical level, which means that a fruitful empirical political science can be of much greater assistance for those interested in constitutional design than for those interested in winning a given election.

The link between the empirical study of politics and constitutional design has three interesting potential consequences. First, the relative importance of an empirical study can be gauged by the possibility that it can contribute to our understanding of policy or of institutional outcomes, which may help winnow the wheat from the chaff in our major journals. The more a particular study helps us understand and predict policy and institutional consequences, the more useful it is for constitutionalism.[26]

Second, such a link argues for more attention to the integrative study of empirical research already completed. There is a myriad of research that remains largely unconnected with respect to major theoretical implications. The time may have come to give more weight and journal space to studies that "clean up" the literature, with a view to developing useful generalizations rather than new findings; this will in turn suggest key areas for further empirical research.[27] Such analysis is likely to be improved by using a constitutional approach.

Third, to the extent that constitutional design requires that we make choices about the ends or consequences that are worth pursuing, we can put empirical research in the context of normative concerns without either denigrating or warping the empirical enterprise itself. In short, the use of constitutionalism to define the political has deeply integrative functions.

One peculiar strength of using constitutionalism to define the political is that instead of imposing an analytic scheme upon empirical data, constitutionalism works from an empirical base. That is, no one has sat down and abstracted a definition to which the real world must then conform. Rather, constitutions are historical facts that rest upon and encode generations of behavior. Although the basics of constitutionalism are now well understood, actual constitutions will vary in content from place to place and from time to time. Thus, the composition of the political is always changing at the margin as constitutional political systems operate. Business corporations come to be, for a time, protected by the due process clause, and then the protection is withdrawn. Constitutionalism has not changed, but the constitution has, and political controversy over such issues becomes the very definition of politics.

What Is *American* Political Theory?

If our intent is to elaborate a discipline that addresses a peculiarly American approach to the theoretical study of politics, it quickly becomes apparent why the birth will be a struggle. American political theory is not just the theoretical study of American politics but is also the study of American theory with its distinctive premises, questions, and methods. This is an important distinction because one premise underlying the argument here is that American political theory is not the simple application of European political theory to the study of American phenomena. Rather, there is a recognizable American political theory, or set of theories, with which European thought overlaps but does not determine. American political theory has a basis that is to a significant degree independent of European antecedents, and this independent base, among other reasons, to a large extent explains why Americans have attempted to develop a functioning *science* of politics while the Europeans have not.[28]

The hypothesis of American particularism is not currently popular among historians, and it certainly smacks of an ethnocentrism that provokes phobic reactions among most intellectuals these days; but in the long run we diminish neither ourselves nor others by attempting to understand what we have done and are doing as Americans. Indeed, understanding ourselves is as important for understanding others as understanding others is for understanding ourselves. The danger of developing a self-satisfied smugness is not the major source of difficulty inherent in the thesis of American particularism, however. Rather, we must avoid the twin but opposite dangers of seeing no significance of American political theory for politics elsewhere or of failing to note the limits of applying American political theory to other peoples in different circumstances. In short, American particularism results in historically original and important contributions by American political theory, but those contributions have limited although definite application elsewhere.

American political theory is not simply political theory written by Americans. For example, one of the most interesting theoretical treatments of American politics was written by a Frenchman—Alexis de Tocqueville's two-volume work *Democracy in America*. Few texts of this type in American political theory are written by Americans or non-Americans; indeed, one might argue that there are no great texts in American political theory equivalent in sweep and depth to the works of Plato, Aristotle, Machiavelli, Hobbes, Montesquieu, Hume, Rousseau, Marx, or Mill.[29] There are, instead, many small texts written by many hands, and a good number of the most important are the products of committees. Moreover, a major portion of American political theory is contained in public documents that speak institutionally rather than philosophically. In the classification of intellectual endeavors, American political theory is a distinct genus within the phylum of political philosophy. Perhaps it would be better to term it a genre, since the kinds of texts that define American political theory differ as a genre from the other texts used in political theory in general.

American political theory can also be viewed as our discourse over a set of institutions and processes that are historically distinctive and important. To this day the British, from whom we split off, do not understand the institution of federalism that we developed as a functioning institution and gave to the world. Americans also invented the institutionalized separation of powers and the mechanistic system of checks and balances. Americans invented the written constitution, modern bills of rights, and declarations of independence. The presidential system, nonparliamentary legislatures, an independent judiciary, popular sovereignty, universal suffrage, mass political parties, organized interest groups, and the constitutional amendment process are just a few more examples of institutions and processes that define American politics, and the discourse about such processes could be seen as defining American political theory.

The American genus might also be defined by a set of values, questions, and issues that underlies, informs, and directs discussion in the texts surrounding our distinctive political institutions and processes. Or it might be defined as an approach to political discourse, an instinctive American preference for reliance upon experience, a pragmatic preference for that which solves problems over that which is merely logical, and an inclination to empiricism coupled with a sense of mastery over our collective destiny that makes political science a natural and persistent goal for American political theory.

Whether defined as a set of texts, a set of institutions, a set of values and issues, or as a distinctive approach to political discourse, American political theory has at its center a tradition of constitutionalism; and this core is both a strength and a weakness. It is a strength, in part, because we are clearer about the limits of political discourse and the nature of politics. It is a weakness because its diffuse, multifaceted character and the large number of texts by which it is carried make it impossible to readily insert American political theory into the broader enterprise of political thought of the world at large. We are partially insulated, some would say distanced, from the rest of the world by our particularism; and at the same time passing this diffuse, demanding tradition on to our children grows more and more difficult.

This preface to a discipline is intended to help ease these problems, to make our tradition of political discourse more accessible to ourselves and to others. The various lists, especially those of texts, are intended to introduce American political theory rather than to close off discussion about material that should be included. Above all, unlike other books that serve as introductions to American political theory, this one is more properly a preface since it discusses a subject that is often improperly taken for granted but that must be consciously brought to the fore if we are to make headway in defining and passing on a discipline of American political theory.

That discipline can now be provisionally defined as the normative, analytic, and empirical study of American texts, institutions, processes, issues, and values derived from and defined by its constitutional tradition. American political theory thus embraces the various types of theory, a variety of phenomena for study, and several quite different methodologies. The mental discipline includes not only becoming competent in these different areas but also the willingness and ability to refuse any temptation to disregard relevant work because it uses a different methodology or focuses upon a different type of data. Ultimately American political theory must strive to be integrative, and perhaps part of the mental discipline it requires is the willingness and ability to take abuse from the several quarters where it intrudes.

The interlocking network of American national and state constitutions as it evolves over time defines the boundary of American political theory. As a result these constitutions serve as the place where we must begin. The study of elections, parties, the presidency, legislatures, public opinion, and so on are part of American political science precisely because our constitutions create a political system that includes, requires, or allows them. Constitutions serve the double purpose of embodying and codifying what we have learned from past behavioral regularities in political behavior, and at the same time the summary of preferred or expected behavior contained in these constitutions helps structure and explain future political behavior. Thus, American political theory must start with the texts of American constitutional documents and the explanatory texts written around these documents, of which *The Federalist* is a prime example.

Certain problems are inherent in the study of
cal texts, however, some resulting from the natur
eral and others from the nature of American politi
ular. The next step in exploring a preface to /
theory, therefore, involves a discussion of textua

Chapter 2

American Political Texts
and Their Analysis

Political theory begins with the analysis of texts, and American political theory has a series of peculiar problems because of the texts upon which it is based. First, constitutionalism defines American political theory at its core, and American constitutional documents are therefore among its central texts. These documents cannot be analyzed in the same way as philosophical texts, however.

Philosophical writing usually aims at pushing thinking and understanding to higher levels or into unexplored regions, and new words or concepts are frequently developed to describe or explain ideas for which our old vocabulary is inadequate; the reasoning is often subtle, complex, and somewhat at odds with currently accepted modes of thought. When we read the philosophical texts from the past that are considered to be outstanding works or "great books," their greatness may affect us to the extent that their contents become part of our present thinking, but there is still a singularity, an originality to the texts that leads us to associate certain ideas or perspectives with specific thinkers. Yet we continue to read these outstanding philosophical works not only to familiarize new generations with the important, distinctive ideas they contain but also because the authors are such good exemplars of how to apply theoretical analysis; their thinking is so profound that we hope to learn even more than we did on our last reading. These thinkers are distinguished by such deep patterns of thought that we can find in their works meaning that seems almost bottomless, and sometimes we rightly conclude that the deeper meanings, which we uncover in a text only after an arduous analysis on our part, were intended by the author to be found only by careful readers. That is, philosophical texts have deeper structures of meaning that are not accessible to casual readers, and elaborate theories of textual analysis have been developed to aid us in finding these deeper meanings.[1]

Viewed as texts, political documents differ from philosophical ones in almost every respect. Political documents in a constitutional tradition by definition are aimed at a broad public, a readership composed of the general citizenry, rather than at a relative few people who are skilled at careful reading. Furthermore, these documentary texts are not primarily supposed to create and present new ideas, although sometimes this is part of their purpose, but to summarize, encapsulate, codify, interpret, reinterpret, modify, extend, or merely celebrate ideas and concepts that are already generally understood and accepted by most citizens. The great texts of American constitutionalism, for example, the Declaration of Independence, the Constitution, and the national Bill of Rights, are great, not because of their originality but because they successfully summarize important ideas and concepts that were the widely accepted core of American political thinking at the time they were drawn up.[2] Therefore the language used in these documents is not usually new or original in meaning but unexceptional and part of the ordinary language of the time. Constitutional documents must be tied to ordinary language because by definition they rest upon the consent of the citizens. If such documents cannot be understood by the citizens, if they contain secret or hidden meaning, then the citizens cannot be said to have given their consent to the texts, and thus the documents are not constitutional. That is, their status as texts rests upon popular acceptance, and anything that seriously interferes with this consent renders the texts politically meaningless.

Furthermore, citizens can approve a political text without seeing all of its possible consequences—consequences that may have been intended as well as unforeseen. For example, not all Americans at the time of ratification anticipated the doctrine of "implied powers" that would be derived from Article 1, Section 8, paragraph 18 of the U.S. Constitution. Despite Antifederalist warnings, many did not understand the "spirit of consolidation" in the Constitution's design. Still, whatever was intended, the words "necessary and proper" could be interpreted in several different ways, and whichever interpretation won was a function of political struggle and not of some hidden meaning. That is, the victory of one reading over another did not rest upon a meaning that an average person could not see as possible, given an ordinary understanding of the language.

In sum, in a constitutional tradition such as ours, political texts that form the core around which our theoretical thinking is built must be read for their commonly understood surface meaning, tend to contain currently accepted modes of thought rather than ideas original for the time, may be singular in the power or efficiency of their expression but cannot be idiosyncratic, are aimed at a general public rather than at a select few, frequently are important to us not because of their depth or excellent expression but because they have been ratified by popular consent, and inevitably have been composed by groups or committees rather than by single authors.

A given document subjected to textual analysis usually expresses only a portion of a coherent theory rather than a theoretical position that is worked out comprehensively. American political theory moreover generally lacks the great philosophical tracts associated with European political theory; instead, we have several assembled and partial texts such as *The Federalist* that not only require a somewhat different form of textual analysis but also require that we face the question of what constitutes a complete text. Finally, texts in American political theory frequently borrow from European texts, but Americans, working from their particularistic circumstances, have tended to use European texts selectively and in piecemeal fashion.

The inclination of Americans to appropriate pieces of European political thinking and to make them part of American political theory raises some interesting questions for textual analysis. When we approach the great European thinkers and try to relate them to American political thought, to what extent should we read the European writings in their own terms as freestanding texts, and to what extent should we read these works in the context of those who originally appropriated and blended them with our tradition?

Americans have written a large number of theoretical books, especially in this century, that derive from empirical or analytic bases or both and either analyze American politics or provide "middle-range theories" that are considered relevant to theoretical discourse about American politics. Textual analysis in these instances requires a grounding in techniques of formal analysis or in techniques of data-based research. Because these books are relevant to American political theory and have been written by Americans they are part of our list of texts to be analyzed, but they force us to enter yet another style of textual analysis.

We can tentatively identify several different kinds of texts relevant to American political theory, each with its own appropriate rules for analysis.

1. Public documents such as the U.S. Constitution that rest upon popular consent for their status as texts
2. Public documents such as Supreme Court decisions that do not rest upon consent for their status as texts but that are still dependent upon public understanding
3. Public writings such as the papers in *The Federalist*, Madison's notes on the Federal Convention, reprinted sermons, and other political pamphlets that explain or critique aspects of American political theory but that are partial or incomplete and must be assembled or incorporated into larger texts for coherence
4. Historical documents such as newspaper editorials, the Jefferson/Adams correspondence, probate-court records in Massachusetts, or voting records that must be analyzed using one of several methodologies not relevant for analyzing books
5. Histories of American political thought such as Forrest McDonald's *Novus Ordo Seclorum*, Gordon Wood's *The Creation of the American Republic*, and Andrew C. McLaughlin's *Foundations of American Constitutionalism*—or more general American histories such as James Truslow Adams's *The Epic of America*, Charles M. Andrews's *The Colonial Period of American History*, and Charles and Mary Beard's *The Rise of American Civilization*—that use techniques of history to assemble meaning from many documents
6. Theoretical works such as John C. Calhoun's *Disquisition on Government*, Herbert Croly's *The Promise of American Life*, Jo-

seph Schumpeter's *Capitalism, Socialism, and Democracy* and Michael Walzer's *Spheres of Justice* that are offered as original and complete texts, including those in philosophy and theology

7. European texts such as John Locke's, *Second Treatise on Government* that have been appropriated to American political theory, at least in part, by earlier generations or whose relevance is such that we continue to relate them to American political theory today

8. Literary works and biographies that speak directly or by implication to American political life, such as *The Education of Henry Adams*, Eldridge Cleaver's *Soul on Ice*, Melville's *Moby Dick*, and Robert Penn Warren's *All the King's Men*

9. Empirical analyses of American politics such as Theodore Lowi's *The End of Liberalism*, Donald Campbell et al., *The American Voter*, and Robert Dahl's *Who Governs?* that build theory on an analysis of data

10. Analytical books by Americans such as James Buchanan and Gordon Tulloch's *The Calculus of Consent*, John Rawls's *A Theory of Justice*, and Hanna Pitkin's *The Concept of Representation* that discuss politics in general rather than American politics in particular but that also offer theoretical analyses, which are obviously of particular relevance to American politics.

Not only does the unusual nature of American political theory require its students to become familiar with a large number of texts with widely varying characteristics, it also requires that they think through their actions as they subject these various texts to analysis. Before these issues can be explored fruitfully, however, we must first understand a bit more systematically the process of textual analysis.

What Is a Text?

When we analyze texts, we are interested in understanding them, in extracting meaning. The meaning of a text is tied to a number of factors, including

1. the denotation and connotation of words,
2. the structured relationship between words produced by the application of rules of grammar,
3. the overall argument or logical progression of implications produced by such meaning and structure over an entire text,
4. the context in which the text was written,
5. the questions we bring to the text.[3]

In order to advance our discussion of textual analysis in American political theory, it is necessary to consider a bit more carefully the first, fourth, and fifth aspects of textual meaning.

Denotation refers to the direct, explicit meaning or reference of a word; connotation refers to the suggested ideas associated with a word or phrase in addition to this explicit meaning. For example, "mother" denotes a female parent, but it also connotes love, care, tenderness, security, and so on. Most words denote more than one kind of meaning, and Hanna Pitkin made this point most exquisitely when she wrote a substantial book that laid out the surprisingly numerous kinds of actions and institutions denoted by "representation."[4] Connotation is even more problematic. Take, for example, the word "red"; it denotes a color with which we are all familiar, a color that can be defined simply by pointing at certain objects such as red delicious apples, fresh blood, and the like. But consider the sentence "She is very red." A literal textual analysis would require that the person signified have skin and hair the color of a ripe red delicious apple, an unlikely meaning. The sentence could connote the equivalent of "She is embarrassed," or "She is a communist." To unravel the denotation and connotation of words and sentences we must consider the broader context of the entire paragraph or even the entire piece of writing. It would also help to know when it was written and who the intended audience was.

If the sample sentence is found in a text written before Karl Marx was born, its connotation of communism could easily be eliminated. Thus, the context in which the text was written may provide much of the information that we will need to understand its meaning. Denotations and connotations will vary over time and from place to place. Take once again the sentence "She is very red." Unless we are sensitive to the use of words at a given time in history, we would miss the connotation familiar to readers of Shakespeare, "Let us make incision for your love, / To prove whose blood is reddest, his or mine," or to readers of Sir Walter Scott, "His blood was too red to be spared when that sort of paint was in request."[5] In these instances "red" implies superior quality or value.

It is especially important when analyzing a text from an earlier historical period, such as from the American founding era, to avoid committing an anachronism—to read back into a text a meaning that was not yet in use or information that could not have been known to the writer or his contemporary reader since the event had not yet occurred. The apparent continuity in American history, largely devoid of the sudden, radical transformations more commonly found during the equivalent span of European history, may sometimes lull us into ignoring the shifts in denotation and connotation that have occurred. To say that linguistic changes have occurred in American political expression is not to imply that earlier meanings cannot be recovered or that ideas expressed with different words might not be fundamentally the same. Yet when we are analyzing American political texts from an earlier era it is essential that we steep ourselves in the writing from that era and remain sensitive to the denotations and connotations of the time rather than cast our own meanings back.[6]

Meaning is not limited to denotation and connotation but also depends upon a broader context with several levels, including how a text was read at the time it was written as well as the questions we might bring to it today. For example, in the United States Constitution we find the following statement in Article 1, Section 8: "The Congress shall have Power to lay and collect Taxes, Duties, Imposts and Excises, to pay the Debt and provide for the common Defense and general Welfare of the United States." Presumably the words "shall have" imply that Congress has these powers but does not necessarily have to exercise them. Congress, however, has historically chosen to exercise all the powers listed to the extent that today we expect Congress to exercise them. Indeed, we now read the passage as *requiring* Congress to exercise these powers as part of their duties.

In this current context, we can then come to this part of Article 1, Section 8, with a variety of questions, including (1) What did the framers mean by "general welfare"? (2) What does the phrase "general welfare" imply for current American public policy? and (3) Is there anything in the Constitution that can be used to justify the creation of a welfare system?

If one asks the third question under the current assumption that Congress has a duty to exercise these powers and if one applies the current usage of welfare, then it is possible to conclude that Congress has a simple duty to create a welfare system. Suppose, however, we answer question one first, and it turns out that "general welfare" was at the time of the founding a linguistic alternative for "common good." Suppose also that the phrase common good was viewed as implying that public policy should seek to benefit the entire population rather than just a part of it, that all parts of the population should have their vital concerns protected, and that the effects on unborn generations should be considered.[7] The answer to the first question would thus imply an answer to the second one insofar as the first answer entails the duty of Congress to frame legislation that attempts to meet these policy criteria. The answer to question one also implies an answer to question three that varies from the answer obtained through a "naive" textual analysis that superimposed today's meanings for words.

The answer would now seem to be that Congress has a duty to exercise its power to protect the vital interests of all parts of the population, which implies the need for a welfare system for those whose vital needs cannot be met through their own efforts. But it also implies the need for a welfare system grounded in the needs of other parts of the population so that it does not threaten productivity by soaking up too much capital, so that it benefits the rest of the population by making welfare recipients more economically self-reliant in the long run and thus more productive to the general economy, so that it not be funded in such a way and to such an extent that it puts a disproportionate debt load upon some of the young and unborn or consigns some of the young and unborn to poverty, and so that it not demoralize the rest of the population either by seeming to benefit those who are not needy or by seeming to neglect those who are truly needy.

An important principle of textual analysis in reading a political document is that the document be taken as a whole rather than read in isolated pieces, but an examination of this piece of the Constitution is still useful for illustrating the way in which the various components of textual meaning interact to produce a complete understanding of the text. The questions we ask, the original denotations and connotations of words, the context in which the text was written and first read, the current context in which the text is read after many intervening political events and decisions since its writing—these aspects interact to help produce understanding.

Textual analysis in American political theory operates essentially in the realm of common sense and experience. A fundamental premise of American political theory is that politics is accessible to the many and that an understanding of the texts defining American politics is attainable for the many. The kind of textual analysis called for here does not require specialists or pedants but individuals who are experienced enough in the reading of American political texts and in the operation of American politics that they recognize the common sense of the situation. Indeed, textual analysis in American political theory requires that we move beyond the written word alone and supply the common understandings that any active citizen should possess.

Cognitive psychologists have long pointed out that much of human understanding proceeds in this common-sense manner. For example, consider the following text: "Mary heard the ice-cream truck coming down the street. She remembered her birthday money and ran into the house." Psychologists have found that most adults and children immediately understand that Mary is a little girl, that she wants ice cream upon hearing the truck, and that she is going into the house to get money so she can buy some. Interestingly *none* of this information is stated in the text; rather, we understand the text based upon our own experience.[8] In the same way American political texts can be read by ordinary people using their experience as citizens. Frequently those individuals who wrote American political texts assumed, even relied upon, a common-sense reading by citizens. Certain words or phrases were common coin of the citizen's realm and were used to elicit a certain response in readers who were also experienced citizens. In applying close textual analysis to readings in American political theory, then, it is important to consider the responses that the authors assumed would be supplied by the reader. In order to develop a sense of the response a text's readers might be supplying, it is important to immerse oneself in the total political writing of the period surrounding the text under analysis.

Underlying the discussion thus far is the intended meaning of the author or authors. Presumably the entire point of textual analysis is to elicit the author's meaning; otherwise, we could save time by writing our own texts and reading them instead. Generally, the meaning of a text appears to be a function of interplay between the author's intended meaning, the words as written, and the reader's appropriation. Each of these three entities plays a role in establishing the meaning of a text, both at the denotative and the connotative levels, and it is not misleading to say that a text is really a combination of the three. Unraveling the relationship between the author, the written words, and the reader is essential if we are to understand fully the makeup of a text and thus the constitution of a complete text.

Ideal, Complete, and Timeless Texts

The purpose we bring to a text carries with it certain implicit questions that the reader hopes to have answered by the written words. A reader may want to determine an author's intended meaning; or a reader may be seeking further insight into a concept, regardless of the author's position on the matter; or a reader may be seeking some understanding or insight into the context surrounding the the writing and thus will read it along with many other writings from the period; or the reader may be seeking the genesis of some current concept, event, or policy as well as a justification for it.

The reader's role in defining a complete text, then, is considerable. The reader's purpose leads to the selection of one piece of writing for analysis rather than another because it seems appropriate and possibly adequate for meeting that purpose. For example, the reader may want to understand the theoretical structure of John C. Calhoun's *A Disquisition on Government*, and thus reading this piece of writing instead of his "Fort Hill Address" would seem to make sense. The reader's purpose thus leads to an initial, provisional closure on the concept of a complete text; if that person's purpose is met successfully by that piece of writing, then the text is complete *for that reader's purpose*. Suppose, however, that one is seeking to understand the manner and extent to which Calhoun's *Disquisition* contributed to southern secessionist ideology; Calhoun's book then becomes only one of many pieces of writing needed to define a complete text. Finally, some readers will be more experienced at textual analysis or know more about the topic under investigation than someone else and may therefore need to read less writing than another in order to meet their purposes. Thus the amount of writing that defines a complete text may be less for one person than for another with the same purpose.

The author also defines a complete text by writing a work that has a beginning and an end. Presumably a book, with its defining covers, satisfies the author's purpose and is thus a complete text from the writer's point of view. Of course, an author might indicate in a given piece of writing that another piece of writing is assumed or contains important parts of the argument and thus identify a complete text that extends beyond one piece of writing. We can speak, then, of an ideal text, one in which the author's intended meaning is always found in the words by any reader. There is perfect singularity and congruence both at the denotative and the connotative levels of meaning between the author and every reader. The piece of writing is a faultless transmitter, and the author is the dominant part of the author/writing/reader trio. The author not only dominates meaning but also dominates or has foreseen the contexts in which the text can be read, the purposes for which it can be read, the questions that will be asked by the reader, and thus the composition of the complete text.

Even though such an ideal text could never exist, some readers may assume this model as they approach a text. The text is a given, and uncovering the author's intended meaning is the only reason for studying the text. One indication that such a model is being used in textual analysis is that the analyst, or reader, treats the author with obvious and continual reverence. Our point is not to reject the ideal-text model; rather, it is

- to show that the ideal-text model is only one way to approach a text,
- to lay bare the assumptions underlying the ideal-text approach,

- to argue that even if the ideal-text approach is used, the ideal text can only be approximated, and
- to alert us to the dangers of assuming a model of textual analysis that may not always be useful, appropriate, or even possible when analyzing a document such as a constitution.

Any given reader may have a single purpose, but over any set of possible readers the odds that they will share the same purpose approach zero. The piece of writing mediates between the author and the reader, carrying a singular meaning from the author's point of view but simultaneously having to stand the scrutiny of a potential set of readers with a set of purposes quite beyond the ability of the author to predict. Unable to predict the possible purposes to be brought to the text in the future, the author cannot create closure for the text by responding ahead of time to these potential questions.

A further problem is that we can know the author's intended meaning only with probability, a result of the inevitable equivocation inherent in language and of the uncertain context in which the author wrote. Anyone whose purpose is to determine an author's meaning must carefully examine the use of words as well as the linguistic-social-political-historical context. At the very least, a careful study of the words in a text must involve the meanings in use when the text was written. Still, we must assume that the author's logical presentation of the argument is sufficiently careful that it cannot be construed in too many ways. With care, the set of possible intended meanings can gradually and confidently be reduced by readers to a fairly narrow range of alternatives.

Do these apparently imposing strictures rule out the possibility that a timeless meaning can be extracted from a text? Certainly not. Many texts will, over time, continue to have a stable meaning, and some will turn out to contain timeless truths of deep importance so that generation after generation returns to them. Timelessness must be established empirically by many readers; only the continued return of readers to the same reading over a long period of time with approximately the same understanding and continued affirmation of its truth will confirm timelessness. In textual analysis neither truth nor timelessness can be established by one reader any more than an author can cause a piece of writing to become timeless through an act of will.

Once again we are led to conclude that a text is a confluence of three elements: an author or authors, a piece of writing, and a reader or readers. The reader defines a text for his or her purpose and thus, by implication, the definition of a complete text; the author also attempts to define. The author's text and the reader's text will probably differ unless the questions they ask are the same and unless the reader's purpose is to uncover the author's probable intended meaning, guided by the author's purpose.

Assembled and Incomplete Political Texts

It is frequently assumed that the United States Constitution is an ideal, complete, and timeless text; but it is not, and was probably not expected to be, a faultless transmitter of the authors' intentions to future readers. For one thing, the Constitution required considerable explanation by Publius and other Federalists using supplemental texts. For another, the document was written by a committee and reflected a number of compromises needed to obtain committee consensus. Some of these compromises resulted in the deliberate use of ambiguous language; others resulted in contradictory textual messages. But most important, the Constitution is not an ideal text because it is an incomplete one.

Although federalism, the division of power among different legislatures, is never mentioned by name in the U.S. Constitution, it is a central organizing principle in the document. Federalism had an important effect on the text; the states are referred to explicitly or by direct implication fifty times in forty-two separate sections of the Constitution. Anyone attempting a close textual analysis of the document is driven time and again to the state constitutions to determine the meaning or implication of the national Constitution. We can therefore say that the national document is an incomplete text without the addition of at least the state documents.

The partial text of the U.S. Constitution requires the addition of other pieces of writing to assemble a complete, or a more complete, text. The components that constitute a complete text depend upon the question that is being brought to it. If we are attempting to puzzle out the intention of the founders on some matter, then the Bill of Rights, the records of state ratifying conventions, the assembled text of eighty-five newspaper articles known as *The Federalist*, other articles and pamphlets written by Federalists and Antifederalists, the notes by Madison and others on the Federal Convention, the Declaration of Independence, correspondence among key actors, and many other sources may be needed in some combination to answer the question brought to the text. At a minimum, the federalism that informs the Constitution makes it an incomplete text, which alerts us to the possibility that incomplete and assembled texts are an important part of American political theory.

The assembled text of *The Federalist* should have alerted us to this possibility long ago, and the texts recently assembled by Bernard Bailyn and Herbert Storing should have made the point obvious.[9] And yet there is another sense, one both more profound and more interesting, in which the U.S. Constitution is an incomplete text. One of the most important passages involving the states describes an amendment procedure. The concept of formal amendment can arise only after the invention of a written constitution to be amended. The idea of an amendment procedure is not only an innovation of great historical importance, it also conveys to a reader of the Constitution the unmistakable message that the Constitution is not yet finished, is not yet complete.

Alexander Hamilton wrote on the first page of the first essay in *The Federalist* that the American political system is an experiment in government conducted by a free people using reflection and choice as opposed to accident and force. Thomas Jefferson said that each generation must add its page to the unfolding story and that the ability of each generation to do so is part of the story's historical significance. At the very least, it was expected that the formal institutions of decision making would require some future adjustment, for it is in the nature of an experiment that one learns from the mistakes that become apparent during its operation.

The United States Constitution would appear, as part of the intent of its authors, to be incomplete. Its lack of completeness is not merely textual, however, because the text will reflect the result of political activity by future American citizens. The incompleteness, in other words, stems not from any theory of textual analysis or from any characteristic of texts in general but from the nature of American political texts grounded in continuing consent. That is, political documents in a constitutional system, since they rest upon the consent of the people, must in principle always reflect the openness and incompleteness of the political process itself. Unlike texts in literature and philosophy, constitutional texts and the political texts generated by the political system created by the constitution are tied to ongoing, unending, political activity. In America, constitutions are permanently incomplete, and unless we are attempting to define the founders' intentions, we are always forced in constitutional analysis to include court cases, legislation, and executive actions from a two-hundred-year political process. Constitutional texts therefore cannot be analyzed separately from the political process that they define and reflect. This more profound sense in which constitutional and constitutionally conditioned political texts are incomplete requires that we treat them differently from literary or philosophical texts.

Incomplete texts require that we assemble texts. Perhaps using the assembled text of *The Federalist* as our model, we think nothing of assembling Supreme Court decisions into case books; of combining documents, essays, speeches, and other writings from a wide variety of sources into anthologies, grouped by historical era, for use in American political-theory courses; or of bringing together essays and journal articles from every possible source into an edited book, as long as the writings deal with the same general topic. The assembled text is an American invention, one for which Americans have a peculiar propensity—a propensity we exercised first and most frequently in American political theory. The danger inherent in such assembling is all too apparent in collections where, for instance, bills of rights from any era and both sides of the Atlantic are printed together, ripped from the constitutions of which they are usually a part, and deprived of their meaningful context; or where only portions of essays and pamphlets are printed in collections, perhaps to contrast a Federalist position to an Antifederalist position, each represented by a text only a few paragraphs to a few pages long; or where passages of only a few pages from a book, essay, or tract written by people of every possible ideological shading and description are brought together as representative of American political thinking.

Any undertaking, no matter how basically sound in principle or noble in intention, can be handled badly. We are forced in American political theory to assemble texts, but we should discipline ourselves to use complete writings as parts of the assembled text and to err on the side of inclusion. For example, if we are going to read pamphlets from a certain era or on a specific topic, we should read most if not all of them. The need to assemble texts in our discipline perhaps excuses our doing so, but we have no excuse for not making them reasonably complete.

Constitutional Texts and Political Behavior

The inherent incompleteness of constitutional texts has a number of important, straightforward implications, but before discussing these it is necessary to examine some of the assumptions underlying constitutionalism. As an approach to politics, constitutionalism assumes that humans can, as Hamilton wrote, use reflection and choice in governing themselves instead of relying upon accident and force. Hamilton's position assumes that there is a quality that we usually call free will, that free people can engage in reasoned, reflective discourse as the basis for deciding on their actions in common, and that in the absence of reflection and choice politics will revert to a process dominated by accident or force or both. Constitutionalism also assumes that humans can design a political process, based upon their continuing, mutual consent, that can effectively structure human behavior in a way that a reasoned, reflective people can predict and approve. In other words, unless one believes that the provisions in a constitution can effectively structure human behavior to move it in approved and predicted patterns, one will never bother to write and approve constitutions.

What is meant by accident and force? Force refers to the use of violence and threatened violence to make humans act in a certain way. Force may arise from the disproportionate wealth, power, and greed of the elite, or it may arise from the numbers, combined strength, and envy of the many. Certainly any form of arbitrary power backed by violence constitutes the meaning that Hamilton had in mind. To define "accident" is a more subtle problem; it probably refers primarily to the accident of birth that gives the elite an advantage in politics. It probably also refers to a political system that only reacts to events and problems, with the result that its policies have an accidental quality to them rather than being guided by the long-term interests of the people and their posterity. Accident may also refer to politics conducted by a people who remain unconscious of their common needs and goals and who, because they remain prepolitical in their lack of participation in politics, are conditioned by the accidents of their environment rather than by their own choices.

Let us for the moment define "action" as singular, conscious, primarily volitional human conduct and "behavior" as patterned, secondarily volitional human conduct. Action thus refers to conduct that has the full attention of the person or persons involved; behavior refers to conduct that lacks the full or conscious attention of the person or persons involved. Behavior can be viewed as patterned because it is in conformity with previous actions in similar situations, and individuals might engage in it anyway if they were paying full attention. In this sense behavior is secondarily volitional; it rests upon prior conscious decisions to act in a certain way. The first time I drove to work in a new city it was an action, since it had my full attention and rested upon direct, active decisions. After several years I drive almost mechanically and thus "behave" rather than "act."

In a constitutional context, it is assumed that most people engage in patterned, more or less predictable behavior because of conscious decisions and actions that they made earlier. The constitutional documents condition what citizens do, not in the sense of determining their actions but in the sense of making most people engage in behavior that falls within certain defined limits. Constitutions do not produce such behavior by fiat or by reshaping people; rather, constitutions create institutions and processes that use natural human tendencies to produce desired results that are predictable in a statistical sense. Moreover, the people know or are supposed to know these results since they consented to them.

With these assumptions it is possible to see how constitutional texts are fundamentally tied to human action and behavior. Constitutions contain institutions that are based upon hypotheses about human behavior. "If we act to structure the process in this way we will produce outcome X in terms of behavioral regularities;

whereas if we act to structure the process that way we will produce outcome Y." Subjecting constitutions to textual analysis requires, in part, that we determine the patterns of political behavior that are expected to result (in a nonnormative sense) from the institutions contained in the document and that we determine the causal hypotheses contained in the institutional design. Preambles and bills of rights also encode preferred patterns of behavior (in a normative sense), not through institutional design but by enunciating goals, values, and hopes as standards by which to evaluate political actions and behavior.

Constitutions never spring *de novo* from the heads of their authors but are grounded upon and are extensions of political patterns from the past. One can thus view constitutions as summarizing, encapsulating, and codifying patterns of political behavior that are natural to a given people at a given time. Decoding a constitution through textual analysis thus involves developing the snapshot it provides of a people and their preferred political patterns. Finally, all texts, like all actions or statements, are themselves units of action or behavior. Constitutions are complex behavioral manifestations that can be read and analyzed in the same way a political scientist can study an election, a legislative roll-call vote, or a particular policy. A constitution is a behavioral unit, which, when studied in conjunction with other constitutions, can reveal, for example, certain regularities of behavior in constitution making, the links between politics and class structure, the relationship of culture to criteria of justice, or patterns in the diffusion of institutional innovation.

Yet, constitutions can never be studied simply as behavioral manifestations. Their entire purpose is to structure a political process, and therefore constitutions inevitably lead us to examine how successful they are at this task. If the offices defined by a constitution are elective, then the electoral process has a function or set of functions, and we can study the process to determine its effectiveness in fulfilling the function. If the constitution attempts to define a legislative-executive relationship, then we should study the actual operation of that relationship in conjunction with the constitution. A constitutional perspective is therefore inherently empirical, behavioral, and normative.

A constitutional perspective is also inevitably historical. A constitution does not define a political system for purposes of preventing change; rather, a constitution defines a set of institutions and processes that are known and consented to by citizens, and the codified, public nature of a constitution requires any proposal for change to undergo a public, consent-based process for approval. Instead of freezing a political system, a constitution institutionalizes change in such a way as to maximize the probability that change will be accomplished through consent-generating public discourse rather than through force or fraud. Thus a constitutional perspective involves the study of constitutional development and change, and the story of constitutional change is the story of a people as they act in history. At any given moment a constitution worthy of the name embodies and is derived from a people's past, roughly defines their current patterns of behavior, and structures future change.

We have reached the point where it is fair to ask what writings a relatively complete, assembled text for American political theory might include. Since the text is partly a function of the question being asked, there will never be one assemblage that is standard for American political theory, although it is difficult to think of a question that would not lead us to include the United States Constitution. Since questions concerning the initial American founding are frequently asked, however, a text that allows us to understand the terms of that founding would be generally useful. Thus it is time to begin the assembly of that text and to illustrate the process of assemblage, by looking first at the development of that important American invention—the Bill of Rights.

Chapter 3

Toward a Complete Text on the U.S. Bill of Rights

The problem of textual analysis, to recapitulate a bit, is composed of two related problems. The second and more obvious one lies in determining the meaning of a text that is sitting in front of us. Those of us who have engaged in this exercise know that the process of uncovering a text's meaning is deeply satisfying—and far from easy. The careful reading of a political text is not simply an exercise in the application of a literary theory but an interesting puzzle that requires logic, imagination, attention to the political process, a sense of rhetoric, an inclination toward sleuthing, an open mind, a dedication to the systematic ordering of evidence, and a certain skill in what might be called "psychological archaeology"— the careful uncovering of the levels of awareness and the layers of experience that might have motivated an author or authors.

When we are in college, someone will hand us a text on which to practice these skills, but in researching American political theory, there is certainly no one to hand us the text, and usually there is no ready-made text anyway. This lack means that we must face the first problem of textual analysis, the part that is usually overlooked or assumed—the identification of the text that is relevant to the question at hand. Solving this problem involves the same skills as, and is often indistinguishable from or merges with, the analysis of the text itself.

The use of bills of rights in our sample textual analysis is not accidental. If the contention is correct that constitutions define the core and range of American political theory, then because American bills of rights almost always stand at the beginning of these constitutions, rights are, in a sense, part of the preface to American political theory. Also, it is difficult to overestimate the prominence of rights in American political consciousness. The idea that Americans have a national set of rights upon which they can call in the midst of political disputation is a commonplace. Lawyers and citizens alike tend to think of the Bill of Rights first, and too often only, when the Constitution is mentioned.

Rights consciousness is highly developed in America, and American political theory must accord rights considerable attention. A logical preface to this large, important topic is to examine the origin of rights in America, and the method I use here is to ask the question, What constitutes a reasonably complete text for any discussion of the origin of rights in America? This method will allow us to ignore the controversies over how to read specific rights and to focus on the general development of rights, about which there is less controversy.

Contending Hypotheses on the Origin of American Rights

Where should we begin? Unlike the U.S. Constitution, in which internal evidence points us toward the state constitutions as part of a complete text, no internal evidence in the U.S. Bill of Rights immediately points us in a given direction. In the absence of such direction we might pose four contending hypotheses, each of which seems to underlie a part of the literature on the U.S. Bill of Rights. Pursuit of these hypotheses offers one way of generating a complete text on the question.

Hypothesis A: The Bill of Rights was the original product of one or a few minds and was created without precedent in 1789.

Hypothesis B: The Bill of Rights was an extension of English common law, and thus the U.S. Bill of Rights was essentially a descendant of English codifications such as Magna Carta (1215) and the English Bill of Rights (1689).

Hypothesis C: The Bill of Rights was written by James Madison to contain the common proposals for amend-

ments made by the state conventions that met to
ratify the U.S. Constitution. Madison did this in
order to satisfy or placate the Antifederalists.

Hypothesis D: The U.S. Bill of Rights summarized the American view of rights that had been developed earlier and codified in the state bills of rights.

We shall explore each of these hypotheses in turn, although the
first two can be taken together since the discovery of any link between the Bill of Rights and English common law nullifies Hypothesis A.

The second hypothesis points us to Magna Carta as the first
common-law document to examine. One way to test the relative influence of Magna Carta on the Bill of Rights is systematically to
count the overlapping provisions. The Bill of Rights has twenty-six
separate rights listed in its ten amendments, and of these twenty-
six rights only four can be traced to Magna Carta, using the most
generous interpretation of the language in that famous document
(see Table 3.1). Looking at it from the other direction, only four of
the sixty-three provisions in Magna Carta appear in the U.S. Bill of
Rights. The lack of overlap is not surprising since Magna Carta and
the U.S. Bill of Rights had enormously different functions. The
former defined the relationship between a king and his barons; the
latter placed limits on all branches of a government vis-à-vis an entire citizenry.

Despite the enormous historical importance of Magna Carta, it is
only a distant forerunner of the U.S. Bill of Rights in content, form,
and intent. Nor is the overlap with the rest of English common law, although important, that impressive. In addition to the four rights that
can be traced to Magna Carta, another right in the U.S. Bill of Rights
can be traced to the 1628 English Petition of Right and two to the 1689
English Bill of Rights.[1] This brings to seven the number of rights
among the twenty-six in the U.S. Bill of Rights that can be traced to a
major English common-law document, although the highly respected
scholar Bernard Schwartz is willing to make such a connection for only
five of these seven rights.

Writers on the English common law tell us that Magna Carta
had to be continually reconfirmed, at least forty-seven times by
one count, because the document was ignored for long periods of

Table 3.1. First Statement of Each Right in the U.S. Bill of Rights

Bill of Rights Guarantee	First Document Protecting	First American Guarantee	First Constitutional Guarantee
Establishment of religion	Rights of the colonists	Same (Boston)	N.J. Constitution, Art. 19
Free exercise of religion	Md. Act Concerning Religion	Same	Va. Declaration of Rights, S. 16
Free speech	Mass. Body of Liberties, S. 12	Same	Pa. Declaration of Rights, Art. 12
Free press	Address to Inhabitants of Quebec	Same	Va. Declaration of Rights, S. 12
Assembly	Declaration and Resolves of the Continental Congress	Same	Pa. Declaration of Rights, Art. 16
Petition	Bill of Rights (England, 1689)	Declaration of Rights and Grievances (1765), S. 13	Pa. Declaration of Rights, Art. 16
Right to bear arms	Bill of Rights (England, 1689)	Pa. Declaration of Rights, Art. 12	Same
Quartering soldiers	Petition of Right (England) S. 6	N.Y. Charter of Liberties	Del. Declaration of Rights, S. 21
Searches	Rights of the colonists	Same (Boston)	Va. Declaration of Rights, S. 10
Seizures	Magna Carta c. 39	Va. Declaration of Rights, S. 10	Same
Grand jury	N.Y. Charter of Liberties	Same	N.C. Declaration of Rights, Art. 8
Double jeopardy	Mass. Body of Liberties, S. 42	Same	N.H. Bill of Rights, Art. 16
Self-incrimination	Va. Declaration of Rights, S. 8	Same	Same
Due process	Magna Carta c. 39	Md. Act for the Liberties of the People	Va. Declaration of Rights, S. 8
Just compensation	Mass. Body of Liberties, S. 8	Same	Vt. Declaration of Rights, Art. 2

Table 3.1. Continued

Bill of Rights Guarantee	First Document Protecting	First American Guarantee	First Constitutional Guarantee
Speedy trial	Va. Declaration of Rights, S. 8	Same	Same
Jury trial	Magna Carta c. 39	Mass. Body of Liberties, S. 29	Va. Declaration of Rights, S. 8
Cause and nature of accusation	Va. Declaration of Rights, S. 8	Same	Same
Witnesses	Pa. Charter of Privileges, Art. 5	Same	N.J. Constitution, Art. 16
Counsel	Mass. Body of Liberties, S. 29	Same	N.J. Constitution, Art. 16
Jury trial (civil)	Mass. Body of Liberties, S. 29	Same	Va. Declaration of Rights, S. 11
Bail	Mass. Body of Liberties, S. 18	Same	Va. Declaration of Rights, S. 9
Fines	Magna Carta Sc. 20–22	Pa. Frame of Government, S. 18	Va. Declaration of Rights, S. 9
Punishment	Mass. Body of Liberties, S. 43, 46	Same	Va. Declaration of Rights, S. 9
Rights retained by people	Va. Constitution Proposed Amendment 17	Same	Ninth Amendment
Reserved powers	Mass. Declaration of Rights, Art. 4	Same	Same

Source: Based on Bernard Schwartz, *The Roots of the Bill of Rights,* Vol. 5 (New York: Chelsea House Publishers, 1980), 1204. Contrary to Schwartz, I attribute more to English common-law documents, the difficulty being that the English version is always somewhat different in intent and application as well as usually less explicit and sweeping in expression.

time, and its contents were at best honored in the breach.[2] Despite the written guarantees for certain rights contained in major documents of English common law, at the time of the American Revolution these rights were either not protected at all or were not protected in England at the level that they were in America.[3]

Even in those instances where protection of a right in England approached that in America, a fundamental difference existed in whose actions were limited. Partly for this reason James Madison said that there were too many differences between common law and the U.S. Bill of Rights to warrant comparison.

> [The] truth is, they [the British] have gone no farther than to raise a barrier against the power of the Crown; the power of the Legislature is left altogether too indefinite. Although I know whenever the great rights, the trial by jury, freedom of the press, or liberty of conscience, come in question [in Parliament] the invasion of them is resisted by able advocates, yet their Magna Charta does not contain any one provision for the security of those rights, respecting which the people of America are most alarmed . . . those choicest privileges of the people are unguarded in the British Constitution. But although . . . it may not be thought necessary to provide limits for the legislative power in that country, yet a different opinion prevails in the United States.[4]

Any investigation of rights in America would need to begin with Magna Carta (1215), the English Petition of Right (1628), and the English Bill of Rights (1689) for several reasons. First, some American rights do come explicitly from English common law. Also, it is useful to read these documents to see how very different they are from equivalent American documents because of the presence of an aristocracy and an established church in England. Having a clear sense of the dissimilarity between the English and American background helps us to recognize American innovations in rights. Finally, these documents serve as a useful platform for explaining the English definition of rights; the English notion was and is different from ours, and familiarity with at least these English documents will make this difference seem less abstract.

At the very least, the attribution of the American Bill of Rights to English common law and its major documents such as Magna Carta must be supplemented; thus it is to documents written on American shores that we must turn if we are to assemble a text sufficient for us to answer the question about the origin of rights in America. Hypothesis B has enough support for us to reject Hypothesis A, and there is initial support for Hypothesis D, but before moving to the last proposition we must first examine Hypothesis C.

The U.S. Bill of Rights resulted from Antifederalist insistence that the U.S. Constitution be amended in certain ways. Seven of the state ratifying conventions passed resolutions containing suggested amendments, and at a critical point in the ratification debate James Madison promised to lead the fight for a bill of rights if the Constitution were ratified. True to his word, Madison introduced nine amendments containing forty-two separate rights on June 8, 1789, and personally carried the proposal through Congress. It is logical to assume that he used the amendments proposed by the state ratifying conventions when he produced his own list. After all, these ratifying conventions had together proposed ninety-seven distinct rights, and Madison needed to address the opposition to the Constitution represented by these proposed amendments. Yet the forty-two distinct rights contained in Madison's nine proposed amendments, listed in the order he gave them as numbers one to forty-two in the table, bear only a modest relation to the rights proposed by the ratifying conventions (see Table 3.2).

Thirty-five of the amendments proposed by the ratifying conventions appeared on Madison's list, but sixty-one did not. Seven rights proposed by Madison were not suggested by any ratifying convention, nor was there a "dense" connection between Madison's list and the amendments proposed by the ratifying conventions, as can be illustrated by using a somewhat crude measure of association. The data on state ratifying conventions in Table 3.2 constitute a matrix that is seven cells wide and ninety-six cells from top to bottom. If we consider only the top forty-two rows of this matrix, the more cells that have an X in them the denser the relationship between Madison's list and the conventions' proposals. Thirty-two percent of the cells are filled (96 out of 294 cells), which does not suggest an especially dense relationship between the ratifying conventions' proposals and Madison's list of rights.

The last conclusion can also be supported by looking at the proposed amendments made by the ratifying conventions that most directly addressed the protection of state sovereignty. Numbers thirty-one, thirty-two, and forty-two through fifty-three seem

Table 3.2. Amendments Proposed by State Ratifying Conventions Compared with Madison's Original Proposed Amendments

	Mass.	Md.	S.C.	N.H.	Va.	N.Y.	N.C.	Madison
1. Power derived from the people					X		X	X
2. Government exercised for the common good					X		X	X
3. Life, liberty, property, and happiness					X		X	X
4. Right of people to change government		X			X		X	X
5. No. of representatives	X			X	X	X	X	X
6. Congressional pay raises					X	X	X	X
7. Religious freedom		X	X	X	X		X	X
8. Right to a free conscience				X	X		X	X
9. Free speech		X			X		X	X
10. Free to write		X			X		X	X
11. Free press		X			X		X	X
12. Assembly					X		X	X
13. Petition and remonstrance					X		X	X
14. Right to bear arms				X	X		X	X
15. Pacifists need not bear arms					X		X	X
16. No quartering of troops in peacetime		X		X	X		X	X
17. No quartering without warrant					X		X	X
18. No double jeopardy		X						X
19. No double punishment								X
20. No self-incrimination					X		X	X
21. Due process of law guaranteed		X			X		X	X
22. Compensate for property taken								X
23. No excessive bail or fines					X		X	X

Table 3.2. Continued

	Mass.	Md.	S.C.	N.H.	Va.	N.Y.	N.C.	Madison
24. No cruel or unusual punishment					X		X	$\underline{X}$
25. No unreasonable search and seizure		X			X		X	$\underline{X}$
26. Speedy and public trial					X		X	$\underline{X}$
27. Told nature of crime		X			X		X	$\underline{X}$
28. Confronted with accusers		X			X		X	$\underline{X}$
29. Can call witnesses for own defense					X		X	$\underline{X}$
30. Right to counsel		X			X		X	$\underline{X}$
31. Rights retained by states or people					X		X	$\underline{X}$
32. No implied powers for Congress		X			X		X	X
33. No state violate 8, 9, 11, or 26 above								X
34. Appeal limited by dollar amount								X
35. Jury cannot be bypassed								$\underline{X}$
36. Impartial jury from vicinity		X			X		X	$\underline{X}$
37. Jury unanimity required								X
38. May challenge any judicial decision								X
39. Grand jury indictment required	X			X				$\underline{X}$
40. Jury trial for civil cases	X	X			X		X	$\underline{X}$
41. Separation of powers required					X		X	X
42. Powers reserved to the states	X		X	X	X		X	$\underline{X}$
43. Limit national taxing power	X	X	X	X	X	X	X	
44. No federal election regulation	X		X	X	X	X	X	
45. Free elections					X		X	
46. No standing army		X		X	X	X	X	

Cont.

Table 3.2. Amendments Proposed by State Ratifying Conventions Compared with Madison's Original Proposed Amendments (continued)

	Mass.	Md.	S.C.	N.H.	Va.	N.Y.	N.C.	Madison
47. State control of militia					X		X	
48. State sovereignty retained						X		
49. Limits on judicial power	X	X			X	X	X	
50. Treaties accord with state law		X						
51. Concurrent jurisdiction for state and national courts		X						
52. No infringing of state constitutions		X				X		
53. State courts to be used as lower federal courts				X		X		
54. Can appeal Supreme Court decisions						X		
55. Defend oneself in court					X		X	
56. Civil control of military					X		X	
57. Trial in state crime occurs	X							
58. Judges hold no other office	X							
59. Four-year limit on military service					X		X	
60. Limit on martial law		X			X			
61. No monopolies	X			X		X	X	
62. Reduce jurisdiction of Supreme Court	X			X				
63. No titles of nobility	X			X		X		
64. Keep a congressional record					X	X	X	
65. Publish information on national use of money					X		X	

Table 3.2. Continued

	Mass.	Md.	S.C.	N.H.	Va.	N.Y.	N.C.	Madison
66. Two-thirds of Senate to ratify commerce treaties					X		X	
67. Two-thirds of both houses to pass commerce bills					X		X	
68. Limit on regulation of D.C.					X	X	X	
69. Presidential term—only eight years					X		X	
70. President limited to two terms						X		
71. Add state judges to impeachment process						X		
72. Senate does not impeach senators					X		X	
73. Limit use of militia out of state		X				X		
74. Judicial salaries not changed					X		X	
75. Add requirements for being president						X		
76. Two-thirds vote of both houses needed to borrow money						X		
77. Two-thirds vote of Congress must declare war						X		
78. Habeas corpus						X		
79. Congressional sessions to be open						X		
80. No consecutive terms in Senate						X		
81. State legislature must fill vacant Senate seat						X		
82. Limit on power of lower federal courts						X		

Cont.

	Mass.	Md.	S.C.	N.H.	Va.	N.Y.	N.C.	Madison
83. Congress may not assign duties to a state							X	
84. Congress may not regulate state paper money							X	
85. No foreign troops to be used							X	
86. State law used on military bases						X		
87. No multiple office holding	X			X	X	X		
88. Limit on bankruptcy laws						X		
89. No presidential pardon for treason						X		
90. President not the commander of the army	X					X		
91. Official form for president's acts						X		
92. No poll tax	X							
93. No suspension of laws by executive					X		X	
94. No separate emoluments					X		X	
95. Judicial system may not be bypassed					X		X	
96. Advisory council for president							X	

Note: The first forty-two rights are arranged in the order used by Madison in his original version sent to the House of Representatives. Going from left to right, the states are arranged in the order that their ratifying conventions produced a list of recommended amendments, from earliest to latest. When an X under "Madison" is italicized, it means that the proposed right eventually was included in the U.S. Bill of Rights.

Sources: The proposed amendments for each state are taken from Merrill Jensen, John P. Kaminski, Gaspare J. Saladino et al., eds. *The Documentary History of the Ratification of the Constitution* (Madison: University of Wisconsin Press, 1976–); Madison's forty-two proposed rights are based upon an examination of the original documents in the National Archives.

to be the best candidates, and only three of these fourteen proposals appear on Madison's list. The density for these fourteen proposals is 46 percent (forty-two out of ninety-one cells), which makes them one and a half times as likely to be recommended by a state as those actually picked by Madison, and about the same ratio relative to the table as a whole (201 out of 672 cells = 30 percent)—suggesting a strong interest in state sovereignty from the ratifying conventions but not from Madison.

The connection between Madison's list of rights and those rights proposed by the ratifying conventions is thus definite but weak. Most of the rights on Madison's list appeared somewhere in the ratifying conventions' proposals but usually on only one or two lists, and these were generally not the rights most desired by the Antifederalists. Still, a complete text for our question would seem to require inclusion of the surviving debates of the ratification conventions, in part to see the manner and extent to which the wordings and concepts are the same and also to become familiar with those proposals not included by Madison.[5]

Madison apparently wished to avoid most of the amendments proposed by the ratifying conventions, but he needed to make some connection with state interests to mollify the Antifederalists. He fastened upon the tactic of exploiting ambiguities in the Antifederalist position. Americans who argued most vigorously against the proposed Constitution offered three different kinds of amendments that were often intertwined and confused. One type was aimed at checking the power of the national government by withholding a specific power; examples included prohibitions on direct taxes, on monopolies, and on borrowing money. A second type of amendment altered an institution in such a way as to weaken it significantly, for instance by making senators ineligible for consecutive terms, by giving state and national courts concurrent jurisdiction, and by requiring a two-thirds vote in both houses for any bill dealing with navigation or commerce. A third type of amendment was suitable for a bill of rights as we now understand it; examples included protection of the rights to speak, write, publish, assemble, and petition (rights that safeguarded the ability of a people to organize politically) as well as prohibitions on self-incrimination, double punishment, excessive bail, and searches without a warrant (rights that defined an impartial legal system).

One can see in Madison's selection process a clear inclination toward the third over the first two kinds of amendments.

In effect, Madison avoided any alteration in the institutions defined by the Constitution, largely ignored specific prohibitions on national power, and opted instead for a list of rights that would connect clearly with the preferences of state governments but that would not increase state power vis-à-vis the national government defined in the Constitution. The discussion about powers and rights was thus subtly shifted to one only about rights.

This finesse upset some Antifederalists who argued that Madison had "thrown a tub to a whale" (that is, he had created a distraction to deflect public attention from the real issue); but it worked well for one critical reason—Madison used the bills of rights attached to the state constitutions as his model. The Antifederalists had difficulty opposing Madison's use of this model, one of their own making, and it was included in their demands. Madison offered the Antifederalists the "paper barriers" he felt were ineffective in existing state constitutions, and the Antifederalists had either to accept such amendments as useful or to admit the truth of Madison's paper-barrier argument.

Therefore, the immediate background for the United States Bill of Rights was formed by the state bills of rights written between 1776 and 1787. Madison effectively extracted the least common denominator from these state bills of rights, excepting those rights that might reduce the power of the national government. Almost every one of the twenty-six rights in the U.S. Bill of Rights could be found in two or three state documents and most of them in five or more.[6]

The state bills of rights typically contained a more extensive listing than the twenty-six rights that came to be included in the first ten amendments to the U.S. Constitution. Maryland's 1776 document listed forty-nine rights in forty-two sections, Massachusetts' document listed forty-nine rights in thirty sections, and New Hampshire listed fifty rights in the thirty-eight sections of its 1784 document.[7] Virginia's (1776) forty-two rights and Pennsylvania's (1776) thirty-five rights came closest to the size but not the content of the national Bill of Rights.[8]

Clearly there is a strong connection between the state bills of rights and Madison's proposed amendments (see Table 3.3). If we look at the matrix formed by the forty-two rights on Madison's list and the seven state bills of rights, 50 percent of the cells in the matrix are filled (173 out of 294 cells) compared to the 32 percent density between Madison's list and the amendments proposed by the state ratifying conventions. Remember that these state bills of rights were written well before the state ratifying conventions made their recommendations. If we construct a matrix using the contents of the state bills of rights and the rights on Madison's list that were eventually ratified as the U.S. Bill of Rights, we find that the percentage of the matrix filled rises to 60 percent, compared with a 36 percent filled matrix when comparing the state ratifying conventions' proposals with the rights actually ratified as part of the national Bill of Rights.

A final comparison between Table 3.2 and Table 3.3 indicates another connection between the state and national constitutions. The listing for the two tables is the same for the first forty-two rights since in each case these are the rights contained in Madison's proposed amendments in the order in which he proposed them. The rights listed after number forty-two vary in the two tables, however, depending upon the actual content of the documents being examined.

In Table 3.3 rights numbered forty-three through fifty-two have a high density (73 percent), and they also happen to be addressed successfully in the body of the U.S. Constitution proper, as are numbers fifty-five, sixty through sixty-five, and eighty-one. In other words, seventeen provisions commonly found in state bills of rights had already been addressed in the body of the Constitution and did not need to be included in the national Bill of Rights. Also, only a few of these provisions from the state bills of rights are directly contradicted by anything in the Constitution. The importance of the state constitutions and their bills of rights for the national Constitution is even stronger than is apparent from an examination of the Bill of Rights alone. On the other hand, if we look at the list of proposals from the ratifying conventions, only eight are addressed in the Constitution proper, and at least twenty-three of the remaining proposals are directly contradicted by provisions in the Constitution.

One final comparison should drive the point home. The average state bill of rights contained thirty-five rights, and among these

Table 3.3. Madison's List of Proposed Amendments Compared with Provisions in the Existing State Bills of Rights

	Va.	Pa.	Del.	Md.	N.C.	Mass.	N.H.	Madison
1. Power derived from the people	X	X	X	X	X	X	X	X
2. Government exercised for the common good	X	X	X	X		X	X	X
3. Life, liberty, property, and happiness	X	X	X	X		X	X	X
4. Right of the people to change government	X	X		X		X	X	X
5. Number of representatives								X
6. Congressional pay raises								X
7. Free exercise of religion			X	X	X	X	X	X
8. Right to a free conscience	X	X	X	X	X	X	X	X
9. Free speech		X						X
10. Free to write								X
11. Free press	X	X	X	X	X	X	X	X
12. Right to assemble	X			X	X			X
13. Petition and remonstrance	X	X	X	X	X			X
14. Right to bear arms		X			X	X		X
15. Pacifists need not bear arms								X
16. No quartering of troops in peacetime			X	X		X	X	X
17. No quartering without warrant			X	X		X	X	X
18. No double jeopardy							X	X
19. No double punishment								X
20. No self-incrimination	X	X	X	X	X	X	X	X
21. Due process of law guaranteed	X	X	X	X	X	X	X	X
22. Compensate for property taken				X	X	X	X	X
23. No excessive bail	X		X	X	X	X		X
24. No cruel or unusual punishment	X		X	X	X	X		X

Table 3.3. Continued

	Va.	Pa.	Del.	Md.	N.C.	Mass.	N.H.	Madison
25. No unreasonable search and seizure	X	X	X	X	X	X	X	X
26. Speedy and public trial guaranteed	X	X	X	X	X	X	X	X
27. Told nature of crime	X	X	X	X	X	X	X	X
28. Confronted with accusers	X	X	X	X	X	X	X	X
29. Can call witnesses in own defense	X	X	X	X		X	X	X
30. Right to counsel		X	X	X		X	X	X
31. Rights retained by states or people						X		X
32. No implied powers for Congress								X
33. No state may violate 8, 11, or 26 above								X
34. Appeal limited by dollar amount								X
35. Jury cannot be bypassed								X
36. Impartial jury from vicinity	X	X	X	X				X
37. Jury unanimity required								X
38. May challenge any judicial decision								X
39. Grand jury indictment required					X			X
40. Jury trial for civil cases	X							X
41. Separation of powers required	X			X	X	X	X	X
42. Powers reserved to states or people						X	X	X
43. No taxation without consent	X	X	X	X	X	X	X	
44. Free elections protected	X	X	X	X	X	X	X	
45. Frequent elections required	X	X	X	X	X	X		
46. No standing army permitted	X	X	X	X	X	X	X	
47. Civil control of military	X	X	X	X	X	X	X	

Cont.

Table 3.3. Madison's List of Proposed Amendments Compared with Provisions in the Existing State Bills of Rights (continued)

	Va.	Pa.	Del.	Md.	N.C.	Mass.	N.H.	Madison
48. No martial law (suspending law)	X		X	X	X	X		
49. No compulsion to bear arms	X	X					X	
50. No ex post facto laws			X	X	X	X	X	
51. No bills of attainder				X		X		
52. Habeas corpus	X	X						
53. Justice not sold			X	X		X	X	
54. Location of trial convenient				X		X	X	
55. Independent judiciary			X	X		X		
56. Recurrence to fundamentals	X	X			X	X		
57. Stake in community to vote	X			X				
58. Equality is supported						X	X	
59. Majority rule is protected	X							
60. Frequent meeting of legislature			X	X		X		
61. Free speech in legislature				X		X		
62. Convenient location of legislature				X				
63. Public office not hereditary	X					X	X	
64. No title of nobility				X				
65. No emoluments or privileges					X			
66. No taxing of paupers				X				
67. No monopolies				X	X			
68. Collective property right					X			
69. No sanguinary laws				X			X	
70. Right to common law				X				
71. Right to migrate	X							
72. No poll tax				X				
73. No infringing of state constitutions	X							

Table 3.3.   Continued

	Va.	Pa.	Del.	Md.	N.C.	Mass.	N.H.	Madison
74. No religious test				X				
75. Support of public worship						X	X	
76. Attend religious instruction						X		
77. Uniform support of religion						X	X	
78. Support of public teachers						X		
79. Time to prepare legal defense				X				
80. Rotation in executive office	X							
81. No multiple office holding	X							
82. Proportional punishment							X	
83. Qualified jurors							X	

Note: The first forty-two rights are those Madison compiled and sent to the House of Representatives; the order is that used in his list. The rest of the rights are those found in the state bills of rights but not in Madison's proposed amendments. When an X under "Madison" is italicized, it means that the proposed right eventually was included in the U.S. Bill of Rights.

Sources: Madison's list is taken from the original documents in the National Archives; the rights in the state bills of rights are based on the documents as collected in Francis N. Thorpe, ed., *The Federal and State Constitutions, Colonial Charters, and Other Organic Laws of the United States*, 7 vols. (Washington, D.C.: Government Printing Office, 1907).

there was a common core of twenty-six rights. Nine of these twenty-six rights were mentioned in at least five state constitutions, four were mentioned in at least six, and thirteen were mentioned in all seven state documents. Every one of these twenty-six rights in the common core of state bills of rights appeared on Madison's list of proposed rights or had already been addressed in the body of the U.S. Constitution. The seven ratifying conventions, however, proposed only seven rights that were common to five or more of their lists of proposed amendments. Three of these seven ended up on Madison's list, and none had been addressed in the U.S. Constitution.

The state constitutions and their respective bills of rights, not the amendments proposed by state ratifying conventions, are the immediate source from which the U.S. Bill of Rights was derived.

A complete text for answering our question therefore must include the state bills of rights, the U.S. Constitution, and the state constitutions. The sheer number of rights in the body of the U.S. Constitution indicates the degree to which bills of rights and constitutions had been blended, which in turn suggests that the background to American bills of rights may include earlier constitutional documents as well. This suspicion is strengthened when we note that both Madison's list of proposed amendments and the version produced by the House of Representatives were designed to be placed within the body of the Constitution. It is probable that the answer to our question, "What is a reasonably complete text for any discussion of the origin of American rights?" is similar to that for the question, "What is a reasonably complete text for any discussion of the origin of the U.S. Constitution?"

The Colonial Background to the State Bills of Rights

Having established the importance of state bills of rights as background to the national Bill of Rights, we might ask about the origins of the state bills of rights. They came from bills of rights written by American colonists. Because of English preoccupation with internal political disorder from 1640 to 1688 and then with French competition from 1700 to 1760, the colonists were left with a surprisingly high level of political independence. In addition to writing functional constitutions between 1620 and 1775, the colonists also wrote many bills of rights, and these colonial documents stood as background to the state bills of rights. A high degree of overlap occurs between a state's bill of rights and the documents written during its respective colonial experience.[9] Examples of such colonial documents include the New York Charter of Liberties and Privileges (1683), the Laws and Liberties of New Hampshire (1682), Penn's Charter of Liberties (1682), the General Laws and Liberties of Connecticut (1672), the Maryland Toleration Act (1649), the Laws and Liberties of Massachusetts (1647), and the Massachusetts Body of Liberties (1641).[10] The last document, adopted a century and a half before the American national Bill of Rights and half a century before the English Bill of Rights (1689) contained sixteen

(62 percent) of the twenty-six rights found in the national document.

Where do the rights in the 1641 Massachusetts Body of Liberties and in later colonial documents come from? Interestingly, these colonial documents frequently cite the Bible to justify their various provisions. There is no more a listing of rights in the Bible than there is in the writings of Locke, Hume, or Montesquieu, but the colonists often looked to the Bible for a moral basis upon which to build political goals and values. Basically, Americans' notions of rights developed from their own political experience as colonists, an experience significantly affected by the peculiar and historically important conditions in which they found themselves.[11]

Primarily, the colonists were a religious people. In attempting to lead exemplary lives they were acutely sensitive to human relationships and believed that these relationships should be based upon God's laws as expressed in the Bible. Furthermore, the religion these people professed emphasized certain values supportive of rights, not the least of which were the notions of a higher law against which to measure governmental actions, personal responsibility for actions, and the equality of all people in the eyes of God.

All humans were viewed as having been made in the image and likeness of God, and therefore a certain equality in value should be accorded every person. Those individuals in government were thus not of a different order from those they governed and did not have inherent prerogatives or rights different from others. A fundamental equality lay in every person's ability to say yes or no to God's grace; from this came the ability to give or to withhold consent for human laws, and in turn the concept that government should rest upon the consent of those governed was a straightforward deduction.

These tendencies were reinforced by the belief in the ability of each individual to read the Bible and to have an independent relationship with God. Not only was there no need for priests to interpret the Bible, but each person was viewed as having an independent will; government could not interfere in this fundamental independence. And since God's law was accessible to every person's understanding, so should the human law be, which was supposed to be in conformity with God's law. By implication, a class of lawyers to interpret earthly law was unnecessary, just as there was no need for a priestly caste to interpret the divine law in the Bible.[12] The process for making and enforcing human laws was seen as susceptible to codification that would treat everyone the same and be understandable to all. These codifications were the first American bills of rights.

In addition to religion, the desperate situation of colonists isolated in pockets scattered along a thousand-mile coastline put a high premium on cooperation if they were to survive. The earliest colony, in Virginia, initially tried a military style of organization, but this soon gave way to a system of eliciting cooperation by treating people well. Moreover, where many of the inhabitants were stockholders in the joint-stock company that owned the colony, the privileges normally accorded stockholders in a corporation led to voting rights and the ability to determine company policy. Since the "company" in America erected its own government, the joint-stock form of organization, where it existed, reinforced the inclinations associated with dissenting Protestantism. Early bills of rights were an effective and efficient means for producing order, stability, cooperative behavior, and economic progress.

Finally, the status of American colonies as economic enterprises, especially as seen from England, tended to emphasize economic output rather than political control as the primary consideration. That a loose political control from England produced the most economic output only enhanced the sense that colonists had of running their own lives. A confluence of circumstances led Americans to develop and to expect a set of rights not found in England, a set of rights characterized by a breadth, detail, equality, fairness, and effectiveness in limiting all branches of government that distinguished it from English common law.

No one represented the disjunction between English and American rights better than William Penn, who, because of his Quaker beliefs, suffered through a trial in England that shocks us today. When he founded Pennsylvania, Penn granted religious freedom, which was lacking in England, as part of a bill of rights grounded in his religion and experiences. He also consulted the existing codes of Massachusetts, Connecticut, Maryland, and Virginia, and possibly because of common religious assumptions his list of rights largely overlapped these earlier codes. His Frame of

Government (1682) contained 58 percent (fifteen out of twenty-six) of the U.S. Bill of Rights; the English Bill of Rights seven years later had only one-third as much overlap (five out of twenty-six—19 percent). English common law did form part of the background to our bills of rights, but in America the common law was exposed to the powerful air of equality and independence that transformed it into a profoundly different American version.[13] The Bill of Rights has a long historical pedigree, but that pedigree lies substantially in documents written by people on American shores.

Contrasting English and American Concepts of Rights

The American view of rights was distinguished from that in Britain by two fundamental conceptual differences; one lay in the way Americans used bills of rights to express community values, and the other lay in the English and American notions of liberty.

The first difference stemmed from the religious background and the tenuous situation of most colonists. When we look at the earliest colonial documents of political foundation, such as the Mayflower Compact (1620), the Pilgrim Code of Law (1636), and the Fundamental Orders of Connecticut (1639), we find that among other things these documents usually involved the self-creation of a people—in the double sense of forming a new people and then of establishing the common values, interests, and goals that bound them as a people.[14] These self-defining or self-creating people were in the habit of providing in later documents updated versions of their fundamental, shared values; such lists of shared values evolved into what we now call bills of rights.

It made sense for a religious people to cite the Bible in a bill of rights. Since the Bible was central to the life they shared, the values they held could be justified by identifying in the Bible where these values were enunciated or implied. As the population became more diverse and less religious, the biblical references might disappear but not the tendency for bills of rights to use admonitory language rather than legally binding terminology. Consider for example the following typical excerpts from state bills of rights:

That the freedom of the press is one of the great bulwarks of liberty, and therefore ought never to be restrained.[15]

That the legislative, executive, and judicial powers of government ought to be forever separate and distinct from each other.[16]

All elections ought to be free; and all the inhabitants of this commonwealth, having such qualifications as they shall establish by their frame of government, have an equal right to elect officers, and to be elected, for public employments.[17]

That a frequent recurrence to fundamental principles, and a firm adherence to justice, moderation, temperance, industry, and frugality are absolutely necessary to preserve the blessings of liberty and keep government free.[18]

These may strike some people as peculiar statements for bills of rights, yet they are all from such bills and use language that is typical rather than exceptional. One can see clearly from the use of "ought" and "should" instead of "shall" and "will" that the language is admonitory rather than legal. One can also easily see how these bills of rights are statements of shared values and fundamental principles; here we are a long way from common law.

Contending Views of Rights in 1789

In 1789, on the eve of the writing of America's Bill of Rights, the following contending positions obtained in the Anglo-Saxon world on the nature of rights. One was associated with the common-law view of liberty derived from medieval society and embodied in Magna Carta. In this view the Crown was limited by the rights associated with the aristocracy in the feudal hierarchy and was attached to the distribution of property. Even though this was the stronger of two strains in common law, it was not part of the American notion of rights.[19]

A second position on rights was associated with the other common-law view of liberty—that all English citizens possessed from their common legal and constitutional past a set of rights that protected them from an arbitrary Crown, especially in the operation of the court system. This position had been read into Magna

Carta, most notably by Sir Edward Coke, even though it was not there; in Coke's view the common law protected all English people against royal prerogative. Because this view was used primarily by Parliament in its struggle with the Crown, rights were not seen as limiting Parliament. Since Americans lacked an aristocracy upon which to rest the first version of common law, the second version was dominant in the colonies; this view gave them no basis for resisting Parliament, however, in its attempts to tax the colonies. Thus Americans were left with the older version of common law, which the Glorious Revolution in England had rendered anachronistic, or they had to use a different grounding for rights than that found in the common law.

Fortunately, the colonists had available a view of rights that they had been using more or less for a century and a half and that was undergirded by theology and rationalist philosophy. In this third position all human law had to be judged in terms of its conformity with a higher law; by implication all branches of government, including the legislature, were limited by this higher law. This premise led to the conclusion that all branches of government were subject to popular consent and that rights were defined as the set of guarantees protecting the free and effective operation of that consent.

Bills of rights, according to this view, were lists of common commitments that protected the operation of popular consent and codified the commonly held commitments that popular consent had already identified. By 1776 the language used to express the rights position had become thoroughly secular: "That all power being originally inherent in, and consequently derived from the people: therefore all officers of government, whether legislative or executive, are their trustees and servants, and at all times accountable to them."[20] Preambles to state constitutions frequently had statements similar to this excerpt from the 1780 Massachusetts document: "The body politic is formed by a voluntary association of individuals; it is a social compact, by which the whole people covenants with each citizen, and each citizen with the whole people, that all shall be governed by certain laws for the common good."[21]

The last two quotations might at first appear to be taken from John Locke, but such language was used in America long before Locke's *Second Treatise* was published. The communitarian, popular-consent approach to rights was initially derived from dissenting Protestant theology as it was applied to the design of political institutions in seventeenth- and eighteenth-century North America. The popular-consent view emphasized the needs of the community and saw all branches of government as limited in their operation by universally shared, unchanging human rights.

The similarity in language to that used by John Locke, Algernon Sidney, and other English political theorists is a measure of the extent to which religion and rationalism influenced political conclusions in late eighteenth-century America. The terms and concepts of Sidney, Locke, Bolingbroke, Milton, and a host of other writers were efficiently blended with that of dissenting Protestantism, and thus a complete text on the origin of American notions of rights must include a number of European thinkers as well.

To illustrate the blend, consider the opening articles in the bills of rights of two prominent state constitutions.

That all men are born equally free and independent, and have certain natural, inherent and inalienable rights, amongst which are the enjoying and defending life and liberty, acquiring, possessing, and protecting property, and pursuing and obtaining happiness and safety.

That all men have a natural and unalienable right to worship Almighty God according to the dictates of their own consciences and understanding.[22]

All men are born free and equal, and have certain natural, essential, and unalienable rights; among which may be reckoned the right of enjoying and defending their lives and liberties; that of acquiring, possessing, and protecting property; in fine, that of seeking and obtaining their safety and happiness.

It is the right as well as the duty of all men in society, publicly, and at stated seasons, to worship the Supreme Being . . . And no subject shall be hurt, molested, or restrained, in his person, liberty, or estate, for worshipping God in the manner and season most agreeable to the dictates of his own conscience.[23]

The language sounds Lockean, but it was also taken from Algernon Sidney.[24] Furthermore, an examination of the writings of

Thomas Hooker and Roger Williams, published well before Locke and Sidney wrote, will illustrate the extent to which religious writers in America had already developed the positions outlined in these quotes and in similar language.

Hooker, Williams, Locke, and Sidney saw all branches of government as limited by rights, a position that was roundly ignored in England during the eighteenth century. Yet neither the religious nor the rationalist approaches envisioned having rights legally enforced by the courts rather than by elections, constitutional revision, or armed rebellion. This important step in the development of American bills of rights was still in the future and to a certain extent would rest upon an accident of history.

Drafting the U.S. Bill of Rights

The American view of rights, derived in part from English common law, undergirded by dissenting Protestant theology, and reinforced by rationalist political philosophy, was essentially developed in the local political arena and codified at the colony-wide level. After independence in 1776 the articulation, codification, and protection of rights continued to proceed first at the state and local levels. It should not surprise us, then, to learn that state and local leaders, not national political leaders, insisted upon a national bill of rights.

The United States Constitution, as originally written, contained a number of rights scattered through the document but did not have a fully articulated bill of rights. The Federalists, including Madison and Hamilton, believed that a bill of rights at the national level was unnecessary and perhaps dangerous.[25] They viewed it as needless for three reasons. First, there were extensive bills of rights already in existence at the state level. Second, the political process defined by the national constitution was viewed as so fair, balanced, and limited that it could not impinge upon rights, and if it did the states could always use their own bills of rights to protect their respective citizens. Third, bills of rights were appropriate to a regime in which there was a separation between the people and their rulers but inapplicable to a republican regime in which the people are both rulers and ruled. A national bill of rights was potentially dangerous for two reasons. First, any list was bound to leave out rights that in the future would be considered important but by their absence imply that they were not protected. Second, since bills of rights were statements of commonly held values and commitments and differences in these values and commitments obtained from state to state, a national bill of rights would either have to contain the least common denominator, thus leaving out rights considered important by many people, or else local and state diversity would have to be ignored by the imposition of nationwide standards and values that were in fact not held nationwide. In either case a national bill of rights would be dangerous to rights and liberty.

These arguments did not convince the opponents of the proposed Constitution, and opposition centered most vociferously upon the lack of a bill of rights. James Madison initiated the proposal for amending the Constitution, but it was perhaps the most lukewarm introduction in political history. The *Annals of Congress*, the early version of the *Congressional Record*, show Madison as saying again that a national bill of rights was unnecessary and dangerous, but since he had promised one, here it was.

Madison, mindful of his own words on the dangers of looking to the least common denominator, nevertheless produced a list of nine amendments containing forty-two rights that constituted the core of most state bills of rights. Madison's proposed amendments were given to a select committee in the House of Representatives, with one member from each state on the committee. The House produced a list with seventeen articles, which the Senate reduced to twelve. A conference committee worked out the differences, and on October 2, 1789, a proposed bill of rights was sent to the states for ratification (see Table 3.4).

It was assumed at the outset of congressional action that the bill of rights would either be placed as a list at the beginning of the Constitution, as was the case with state bills of rights, or else scattered through the body of the Constitution proper, as Madison proposed. The Connecticut delegation, however, insisted that the rights be appended at the end of the document as a set of explicit amendments to reflect their true status. Placing them in the body of a document ratified only with great difficulty implied the need to go through the entire ratification process again, but treating them as amendments did not require having to change any wording in the Constitution per se.

Roger Sherman's proposal to place the rights at the end instead of scattering them throughout the document as Madison wanted turned out to be fateful, since listing the rights together at the end gave them a prominence and a combined status over time that otherwise would have been lost. Placing the Bill of Rights at the end, rather than at the beginning as the states preferred, had an unnoted yet historically important effect on the language of the proposed rights.

The lists of rights proposed by the various states in almost every case used the admonitory "ought" and "should" rather than the legally enforceable "shall" and "will," with which we are now familiar. Madison, intending to place the rights in the body of the Constitution, used the constitutionally proper "shall" and "will." Initially the House of Representatives' version used a mixture of admonitory and legally enforceable language, but when the House select committee agreed to accept Sherman's proposal to place the Bill of Rights at the end as amendments, it was necessary to change the wording to legally enforceable language since a "shall" cannot be amended with an "ought."

Without this change in language occasioned by the placement of the Bill of Rights at the end rather than at the beginning of the Constitution, it is difficult to see how American rights could have developed as they did or how the Supreme Court could have emerged as the definer and protector of legal rights. The change in wording was due entirely to the placement of the Bill of Rights, not to any philosophy of American rights theory as of 1789. Later developments in American theories of rights would be heavily affected and conditioned, in short, by a historical accident.

It took two and a half years for the necessary three-fourths of the states to ratify ten of the twelve proposed amendments to the Constitution, which together are now known as the Bill of Rights. Massachusetts, Connecticut, and Georgia did not ratify these amendments until the sesquicentennial celebration of the Constitution in 1939. That the process took so long, that it failed to elicit ratification by all the states, and that two proposed amendments failed to receive the necessary three-fourths support indicate some controversy in state legislatures. Much of the controversy stemmed, as Madison had predicted, from

Table 3.4. Madison's Proposed Amendments Compared with Later Versions

	Madison's Version	House Version	Senate Version	Sent to States	Ratified
1. Power derived from people	X				
2. Government exercised for common good	X				
3. Life, liberty, property, and happiness	X				
4. Right of people to change government	X				
5. No. of representatives	X	X		X	
6. Congressional raises	X	X	X	X	
7. Religious freedom	X	X		X	X
8. Right of conscience	X	X			
9. Free speech	X	X		X	X
10. Freedom of written expression	X				
11. Free press	X	X		X	X
12. Assembly	X	X		X	X
13. Petition and remonstrance	X	X		X	X
14. Right to bear arms	X	X	X	X	X
15. Pacifists—no arms	X	X			
16. No quartering in peacetime	X	X	X	X	X
17. No quartering without warrant	X	X	X	X	X
18. No double jeopardy	X	X	X	X	X
19. No double punishment	X				
20. Self-incrimination	X	X	X	X	X
21. Due process of law	X	X	X	X	X
22. Compensate for property taken	X	X	X	X	X
23. Excessive bail or fines	X	X		X	X
24. No cruel and unusual punishment	X	X		X	X
25. No search and seizure	X	X	X	X	X
26. Speedy and public trial	X	X		X	X
27. Told nature of crime	X	X		X	X
28. Confronted with accusers	X	X		X	X
29. Witnesses for defense	X	X		X	X
30. Right to counsel	X	X		X	X
31. Rights retained by people	X	X	X	X	X

Table 3.4. Continued

	Madison's Version	House Version	Senate Version	Sent to States	Ratified
32. No implied powers for Congress	X				
33. No state violate 8, 9, 11, or 26 above	X	X			
34. Appeal limited by dollar amount	X	X			
35. Jury cannot be bypassed	X	X	X	X	X
36. Impartial jury from vicinity	X		X	X	X
37. Jury unanimity	X	X			
38. Right to challenge judicial decision	X	X			
39. Grand jury	X	X	X	X	X
40. Jury trial for civil cases	X	X	X	X	X
41. Separation of powers	X	X			
42. Powers reserved to states	X	X	X	X	X

Note: The rights are arranged in the order used by Madison in his June 8, 1789, version sent to the Committee of Eleven of the House of Representatives (the committee was composed of one member from each of the eleven states that had ratified the Constitution by that date).
Source: This table is based upon an examination of the original documents in the National Archives.

different expectations from state to state. Some states wanted more or different rights; others wanted fewer. Perhaps we should be surprised that any coherent bill passed at all.

Toward a Complete Text on the Origins of American Bills of Rights

The discussion on rights could continue at great length, but we have gone far enough to make a provisional list in answer to our question, "What constitutes a reasonably complete text for any discussion of the origin of rights in America?" Thus I offer an assembled text of public, political documents that should be addressed, at a minimum, to deal with this question.[26]

Magna Carta (1215)
Letters Patent to Sir Humphrey Gilbert (1573)

Laws and Orders Concluded by the Virginia General Assembly (1624)
Petition of Right—England (1628)
Pilgrim Code of Law (1636)
An Act for the Liberties of the People—Maryland (1638)
Maryland Act Concerning Religion (1639)
Fundamental Orders of Connecticut (1639)
Massachusetts Body of Liberties (1641)
The Laws and Liberties of Massachusetts (1647)
Acts and Orders of 1647—Rhode Island
Connecticut Code of Laws (1650)
An Act Concerning Our Liberties—Massachusetts (1661)
The Charter of Connecticut (1662)
The Charter of Rhode Island and Providence Plantations (1663)
General Laws and Liberties of Massachusetts (1672)
Habeas Corpus Act—England (1679)
Laws and Liberties of New Hampshire (1682)
Penn's Charter of Liberties (1682)
New York Charter of Liberties (1683)
Bill of Rights—England (1689)
Resolves of the Stamp Act Congress (1765)
Appeal to the Inhabitants of Quebec (1774)
Declaration and Resolves of First Continental Congress (1774)
Rights of the Colonists (1774)
Second Declaration of the Continental Congress (1775)
Virginia Declaration of Rights (1776)
Declaration of Independence (1776)
Pennsylvania Declaration of Rights (1776)
Delaware Declaration of Rights (1776)
Maryland Declaration of Rights (1776)
North Carolina Declaration of Rights (1776)
Massachusetts Bill of Rights (1780)
New Hampshire Bill of Rights (1784)
Northwest Ordinance (1787)
Constitution of the United States (1787)
Amendments Proposed by Pennsylvania Ratifying Convention (1789)
Amendments Proposed by Massachusetts Ratifying Convention (1789)

Amendments Proposed by Maryland Ratifying Convention (1789)

Amendments Proposed by South Carolina Ratifying Convention (1789)

Amendments Proposed by New Hampshire Ratifying Convention (1789)

Amendments Proposed by Virginia Ratifying Convention (1789)

Amendments Proposed by New York Ratifying Convention (1789)

Amendments Proposed by North Carolina Ratifying Convention (1789)

Madison's Proposed Amendments (June 8, 1789)

Report of the House Committee of Eleven (July 28, 1789)

Amendments Passed by the House (Aug. 24, 1789)

Amendments Passed by the Senate (Sept. 9, 1789)

Amendments Passed by Congress and Sent to States (Sept. 25, 1789)

U.S. Bill of Rights (1791)

The list of relevant documents is impressive although it is not even close to including all the primary sources. Dozens of major pamphlets, tracts, and essays were written about rights during the 1780s alone, and these must be consulted to help us understand how words were used and how intelligent and informed people of the time actually thought about rights. Then there is a substantial list of secondary sources covering works from the common law to discussions of American politics in the 1780s—all of which help us understand better the Bill of Rights.

One cannot sit down and analyze the meaning of the Bill of Rights as one can a poem—in splendid isolation. The Bill of Rights is a partial text because the Constitution that it amends requires inclusion of the state constitutions to be completed, and this makes the state bills of rights part of American rights. And, just as there are many rights in the body of the U.S. Constitution that must be considered part of the national "rights package," so too are there many rights in the bodies of the state constitutions that are part of the total rights package of our founding.

Of special interest is the list of proposed rights that Madison introduced in Congress since it raises a number of questions about the intentions of the founders. Madison's version, like the state bills of rights and their colonial precursors, seems to say that the most fundamental right is to be subject only to laws to which one has consented through participation in a fair political process; all other rights appear ancillary to this most fundamental right.[27] Given such an understanding, the rights in the first amendment are not simply individual rights in the view of the founding generation but rights that are required for the people to organize themselves to control the political process. The right to communicate ideas freely, to criticize the government, to communicate through speech and press for purposes of creating political organizations, to assemble in groups and in meetings for purposes of organizing, to communicate the results of meetings, to tell those in government what is expected in the way of legislation—these aspects of the democratic process require the specific rights of speech, press, assembly, and petition. These rights are thus not necessarily ends in themselves but may be the means to an end: the popular control of government.[28] Reading a more complete text presents us with interpretations that would be lost with a naive reading of an isolated text.

The primary documentary text assembled here is generated by a particular question, but many questions can be asked about rights, just as there are many ways to use the works in the text just assembled. The question we used to generate the list of documents in our text is essentially a historian's question. It is worth considering how the same list might be approached by nonhistorians since many of the arguments over rights stem from the differing goals brought to a text.

Attitudes toward Texts on Rights

Spending time on a text for the Bill of Rights allows me to illustrate a final, crucial aspect of textual analysis—although the question is the basis for assembling a text, how we treat the resulting text is related to certain attitudes we bring to it. The point will become clearer after considering the possible meanings that underlie the word "right." Essentially a right is a claim made by one person or

group against another person or group.[29] It is a claim that I ar
tled to a certain kind of treatment by others.

General Definition: A right is a claim made by A against B. Such a
claim may result in any one of several types of action—for example,
the claim may be that someone owes me a certain positive action,
that someone must do something I ask; or it may be the negative
claim that someone else must not do something I ask. The claim
might be that a person must act toward me in a certain fashion
even if I do not ask. The claim might be that I may act in a certain
way or else that I may be forgiven for not acting in a certain way.

Regardless of the nature of the relationship between A and B
that the right defines, of critical importance is the grounding or
justification for the claim. Historically, a number of grounds have
been advanced for a right.

1. *Right as Privilege*: the claim that a person or persons must act
   in a certain way toward me as a result of a position that I hold
   (such as those in a given class, caste, social position, or political post)
2. *Right as Duty*: the claim that a certain person must act in a certain way toward me as a result of a position that the person
   holds (such as parent to child, king to subject, or doctor to
   patient)
3. *Right as Promise or Contract*: the claim that a certain person
   must act in a certain way toward me as a result of a mutual
   agreement that we have reached
4. *Civil Right*: the claim that a certain person must act in a certain way toward me as a result of a law, edict, or dispensation
   made by a mutually recognized superior that I be so treated
5. *Common Law Right*: the claim that a certain person must act in
   a certain way toward me as a result of our both being English
   (or American, or Canadian) with a common legal and political
   tradition
6. *Natural Right*: the claim that a certain person must act in a certain way toward me as a result of our both being human
   beings

These are some of the patterns of justification for rights that a
historian would uncover in answer to the question, "How have

rights been justified in Anglo-American history?" That is, a historian will seek to uncover claims that were actually made, by whom, against whom, on what grounds, and at what time. The historian will seek to recreate and to understand the process whereby the claim came to be made and the subsequent effects these claims had. All claims are treated as historical artifacts, so the potential truth of any claim is tied to its congruence with an accurate retelling of events in a defensible sequential ordering.

Thus, the claim that one person has on another as a result of holding a certain position can be confirmed to the extent that the historian can verify which people did in fact hold the positions they said they did and that people of that time and in that culture did have a set of expectations attached to the respective positions; but the historian, as historian, has nothing to say about whether the justification is adequate and worth heeding. The historian can likewise confirm a promise, a contract, a law, a common nationality, or a common humanity, but history as a discipline cannot affirm or deny the truth of any justification for a rights claim. Historians are free to praise or blame and to extract meaning, but these activities are human reactions, not the stuff of which historiography is made. In sum, the historian's attitude toward any text is such that its truth is a function of the facts the record will bear and nothing more.

Empirical political theorists, or political scientists, have a related attitude toward texts. They will ask what claims were made, by whom, against whom, on what grounds, and with what effect; but the political scientist will go further and examine many instances of rights claims in a search for causal patterns that systematically link circumstances with claims and for systematic, predictable effects that such claims might have on human behavior. All claims are thus treated as independent or dependent variables, and the potential truth value any given claim might have is of no interest. Truth is instead related to adequate empirical evidence for regularities in human behavior. Political scientists, like historians, may praise, blame, accept, or reject a given claim, but they cannot do so on any grounds related to their form of inquiry. For political scientists, texts contain data, not truth.

A legal scholar will ask about the status of any rights claim in the context of the relevant laws, cases, and documents. Claims will be examined in terms of their connection to precedent, with principles stated in relevant texts, with principles that are logically implied by relevant texts, or with principles of justice that bring order to widely accepted but diverse principles inherent in the relevant texts. Rights claims tend to be treated as hypotheses about the order or logic that may be found in the relevant texts, and thus the truth of a rights claim is discoverable by reference to these texts but is also limited by their content.

An analytic political theorist will seek out the precise linguistic meaning of rights claims, the logical sense such claims make, and the logical implications they entail. An analytically inclined theorist in part analyzes how rights claims are used by those who make them and by those who study them, with an eye to precision, consistency, usefulness, connotation, and overall coherence. All rights claims are treated as objects of analysis with greater or lesser utility but with no inherent truth value. Truth is related to the logical validity of deductions, and utility as a standard of value has no relationship to truth.

Much of the material in this book falls under the heading of analytic political theory. The title ambiguously implies a concern with analysis, or with pretheoretical analysis, as Charles Hyneman called it, rather than with political science or philosophy. Yet the argument in chapter 1 suggests that the term "political theory" can stand for a combination of empirical, analytic, and normative theory, and it is on the matter of rights that Americans face most squarely the need to move to political philosophy.

A political philosopher will explore the sense that rights claims make in terms of human needs or aspirations, the principles of morality, and the goals and purposes of political organization. Such claims will be examined for revelations about human nature, the good political order, and the adequacy of political institutions. All rights claims are viewed as having potential truth value, and it is the truth value upon which analysis focuses.

Our investigation of a text for analyzing American rights has led us to one of the central and enduring problems in American political theory—the manner and extent to which the enterprise includes a normative core. Recent debates about the relative importance of "virtue" for the operation of our institutions, both at the founding and in the current behavior of our legislators, are a manifestation of the issue. Debates over the extent to which the Constitution rests upon "republican" theory (that is, upon a virtuous people and even more virtuous leaders) or upon "enlightenment" principles (that is, upon principles of design that will produce certain political consequences regardless of the virtue of the actors) are another manifestation. Debates between those who wish to unleash market forces by minimizing governmental interference in our lives and those who see a need for forming civil behavior through regulation are to a certain extent replaying the Federalist/ Antifederalist debate.

How we assemble a text, then, is affected by the question we ask; and both the question and the use we make of the text assembled to answer the question are affected by the attitude we bring to the text. There is no preferred set of questions, no superior approach. American political theory not only has room for these perspectives on rights just described, in the end the nature of our discipline requires that the various approaches must be used and integrated. The purpose of the discussion here is not to establish a litmus test for judging the utility of research but to help those who engage in American political theory become more conscious of their assumptions.

The Bill of Rights since 1792

Although this book is only a preface to American political theory and not a summary of its history, the story of American rights is ongoing and requires further comment. The narrative does not have an ending but an expanding and changing horizon.

Passage of the national Bill of Rights did not really bring change at first; the states were still considered the primary protectors of rights. Only in the early twentieth century, well after the passage of the Fourteenth Amendment, did the Supreme Court begin to use the national Bill of Rights to protect rights in a systematic fashion. One major effect the Bill of Rights did have during the nineteenth century was to lead drafters of state constitutions to recast the language of their bills of rights into the legally binding form using "shall" and "will." With their longer lists of rights and strengthened language, most states were ahead of the national government in the development of rights, although nowhere did the breadth and depth of protection approach current levels.

Two broad developments have occurred during the twentieth century. The first has been the expansion of national rights, as interpreted by the Supreme Court, to an unprecedented degree. We have come to take these rights so much for granted that we forget how recently they have been expanded. The second development has been the application of the Bill of Rights against the states through use of the due process clause of the Fourteenth Amendment. Both developments were made possible by the legally enforceable language inserted in the national Bill of Rights in 1789.

Scholarship and publicity surrounding the second broad development left the impression that rights at the state level were not well protected and that the national government had forged ahead in rights protection, but this perception was not completely true. The problem was not that rights lagged in the states but that diversity in rights existed among the states. Many or most states already protected rights at a level required by the Supreme Court, but ten to fifteen states clearly trailed behind. The net effect of federal action has been to establish a "floor" in American rights; that minimum guarantee is still exceeded by many states.

Active expansion of rights by the Supreme Court, as much as it was needed, had the effect of temporarily eclipsing the development of rights in the states, but that may be changing. In recent years there has been a trend toward "rediscovering" an independent constitutional law at the state level with respect to rights, especially in those states where state bills of rights are stronger and broader in definition than the Bill of Rights.[30]

We now rely primarily upon the courts to protect rights, not a bad thing in itself, but it results in the tendency to focus attention upon court cases and thus upon rights piecemeal instead of upon bills of rights and the general principles they embody. There is an advantage in viewing rights as expressions of fundamental commitments by a people, as the grounding for democratic institutions, and thus as an essential part of the total political process in a constitutional order.[31]

Consider how much of the material that has been uncovered by this discussion of rights in America would not have been uncovered by a textual analysis that worked solely from the text of the

U.S. Bill of Rights. American political theory works from texts that force us to consider explicitly the components of a complete text; this in turn pushes us into a historical approach to American politics. Just as a preface to American political theory must discuss the matter of textual analysis, so too must it discuss the use and misuse of history. We turn now to a history of the study of American political theory during the twentieth century as a means of discussing the complexities of historical analysis.

Chapter 4

The Use of History in American Political Theory

To focus on the Bill of Rights in an attempt to build a complete text illustrates the importance of historical perspective for textual analysis in American political theory, but at the same time it demonstrates the limits of historical analysis. On the one hand the search for a complete text requires that we study historical antecedents as well as the historical and symbolic context surrounding a piece of writing; on the other hand even when we have constructed a reasonably complete text, history cannot help us much in deciding what we should do with that text. The latter task would seem to require a turn to philosophy, but professional philosophy over the past five decades has increasingly tended to avoid normative discourse of the kind that is useful to political theory. To the extent that philosophy has dealt with political philosophy, historically grounded discourse has given way to an abstract, logical analysis with limited application to the texts that might be assembled on American political theory.[1] Further, when philosophers discuss normative issues today they either tend toward an analysis of the possible meanings of words like "good" or else focus narrowly only on an analysis of single issues, such as abortion or capital punishment. Even discussions of rights tend to be reduced to analyses of the possible meanings of "rights claims." Such discussions studiously avoid any language that might imply that rights are actual entities with an existence grounded in human experience.[2]

Thus, at the very time that historians and political scientists working in American political theory have started to create, if not a convergence in perspective, at least a parallel discourse in which there is agreement upon the major questions, philosophy offers no help in dealing with these questions because the intellectual tools and categories increasingly used by academic philosophers prevent mutual discourse. Historians and political theorists still feel comfortable speaking to each other because both sides continue to have an interest in politics. Philosophers, however, persist in adopting methods and categories that are not only apolitical but increasingly antipolitical.

American history has become increasingly empirical, working from facts rather than from grand theory, and this trend has made American historians more interested in politics and more adept at analyzing politics than their European counterparts. Philosophy, however, has become more and more "Europeanized" in its methods and aims, with the result that the problems and issues that students of American political theory must confront are not explored. Politics looks too "messy," too contingent, and too imperfect for American academic philosophers. It has now reached the point that anyone who studies political philosophy in American philosophy departments is looked down upon—as engaged in a not altogether savory enterprise. Graduate students interested in political philosophy in general, and American political theory in particular, now either move to political science departments or find a different interest to pursue in philosophy.

American history, on the other hand, has become increasingly interesting and helpful to students of American political theory. Perhaps because American political theory has been so obviously and continuously connected to ongoing political processes and discourse, not out of accident but by its very nature, theoretical discourse about American politics seems to have become inherently inseparable from the study of American history; in contrast, the study of European political philosophy, centered on great texts more often than not written by men outside the political process, can more easily proceed in splendid isolation from history. As those scholars in political science departments work to advance American political theory, those who are writing in American history will become more rather than less important to them; therefore, the story of the study of American history over the past half century is an important part of the preface for understanding the nature and limitations of the questions that currently dominate American political theory.

An Evolving View of the American Founding

Traditional political theory is built upon a close analysis of texts, which provides its students with the intellectual discipline, insight, and perspective needed to develop a comprehensive, integrated view of politics. Historians, on the other hand, use texts more as examples of broader intellectual trends and view them as providing only part of the information required to describe and explain historical events and developments. One branch of history, the history of ideas, comes closest to traditional political theory in its approach, but the history of ideas still emphasizes the origin, elaboration, and diffusion of ideas; political theory focuses upon the content and implications of the ideas themselves.

American political theory is the one area in which historians and political theorists still plow common ground and speak regularly to one another. Each discipline brings its own tools and preoccupations, and discussions sometimes produce bewilderment or irritation, but historians and political scientists regularly read and review each others' work in American political theory. This connectedness is of interest because since World War II both historians and political scientists have engaged in a sustained, evolutionary reevaluation of American political thought that has moved both sides to a new set of questions that both unites and divides them.

The 1940s found those working on American political thought in political science departments essentially to reflect the viewpoints of historians, and historians for the most part were using a curiously nonhistorical framework for discussing the Constitution. Despite the seminal prewar work by men like Andrew C. McLaughlin and Charles M. Andrews, which illustrated the manner and extent to which the Constitution was beholden to colonial developments, the standard post-war discussion of the Constitution treated it almost as a free-floating phenomenon resulting from events beginning, at best, around 1763.[3]

The literature of the 1940s was dominated by two assumptions or theses, one of which had been advanced by the progressive historians, who were more interested in explaining the present than the past. They viewed politics as a process in which legal and philosophical abstractions masked the real forces underlying history and believed that ideas were secondary to, and the result of, economic and geographical circumstances. Frederick Jackson Turner, Charles A. Beard, and Vernon L. Parrington were most prominent in this group.[4] Charles Beard advanced this first thesis most forcefully when he argued that the founders were motivated primarily by economic considerations, and Parrington softened but generalized Beard's view to cover all of American political thought. The dominance of the economic interpretation made analysis of colonial contributions seem unnecessary, and historians made slow progress until the extreme version of Beard's thesis was discredited in the 1950s. Ironically, with the demise of naive economic determinism, analyses of economic and social influences in American political history flowered and became richer, more concise, and more convincing.[5]

The second thesis or assumption maintained that American political thought was essentially derived from the philosophy of John Locke. Carl Becker and Louis Hartz were most prominent in popularizing the position. Becker was positive in his assessment of Locke's influence when he argued that Jefferson simply copied Locke in the Declaration of Independence, but Hartz decried Locke's domination of American political thought since it resulted in America's being hopelessly individualistic, materialistic, and capitalistic.[6] Agreement on Locke's influence was so widespread that it crossed ideological lines and became for a time one of the strongest orthodoxies in American intellectual history.[7] A few, like Vernon Parrington, discussed the possible influence of other European thinkers; but by and large the U.S. Constitution was viewed either as an economically grounded document that did not flow from an existing theory or as the result of a wholesale transfer of Locke's ideas—with Locke used as ideological window dressing or as a remedy for the lack of any coherent American political thought.

In addition to the works of Beard, Parrington, Becker, and Hartz, courses in American political thought in the late 1940s were also likely to use in some combination the writings of Charles McIlwain, Arthur M. Schlesinger, C. Edward Merriam, Max Farrand, Allan Nevins, and Merrill Jensen.[8] Otherwise, courses in American political thought worked from several collections of primary documents—mainly those of Max Farrand, Jonathan Elliott, Paul Leicester Ford, and Francis N. Thorpe.[9] If any feature distinguished the teaching of American political thought by political scientists as opposed to historians it was the greater inclination by the former to introduce a strong dose of legalism, usually through the use of Edward S. Corwin's many books and articles as well as through a case book of Supreme Court decisions.

The peculiarity in this literature and in the use made of primary documents lay in an almost grim determination to avoid discussion of American political theory as defined in chapter 1. Instead, American political *thought*, often viewed as ideology, was surveyed as part of American culture; Vernon L. Parrington's widely used *Main Currents in American Thought* was utterly typical. Note the absence of "political" in its title and the use of "thought" rather than "theory." Parrington was a professor of English, and his dedication to American thought rather than to American political theory is illustrated by his encyclopedic survey's having little discussion of James Madison yet including passages on the satires of John Trumbull, Francis Hopkinson, and Jonathan Odell as well as a long final section in Book 3 on "The War of Belles Lettres." Parrington does have a section on Alexander Hamilton drawn from original documents including *The Federalist*, but a quotation from that section will illustrate how he used such material.

In elaborating a system of checks and balances the members of the convention were influenced by the practical considerations of economic determinism more than by the theories of Montesquieu. They were realists who followed the teachings of the greatest political thinkers from Aristotle to Locke in asserting that the problem of government lay in arranging a stable balance between the economic interests of the major classes. The revolutionary conception of equalitarianism, that asserted the rights of man apart from property and superior to property, did not enter into their thinking as a workable hypothesis.[10]

Parrington goes on to cite Madison at some length in a passage in which Madison presents a series of theoretical propositions giving part of a theory for checks and balances. But Parrington misconstrues Madison's theory as merely an ideologically grounded attempt to protect the wealthy, ignores the part of the theory that does not fit an economic or elitist interpretation, and then proclaims that such a "conception of the natural sovereignty of the landed interest with its stake-in-society theory of political rights America inherited from England." Edmund S. Morgan is only one of many scholars who have shown Parrington to be wrong in this last respect. Morgan convincingly argues that the way in which Americans view sovereignty, and the way sovereignty is codified in our constitutions, is one of the fundamental differences between American and English political thought.[11] Still, in the 1940s it was assumed that if Americans had a thought during their political history it originated in England. The centerpiece of American political theory—*The Federalist* by Hamilton, Madison, and Jay—was typically used in piecemeal fashion to buttress ideological debate instead of as a text in political theory.[12]

The 1950s saw a move toward a new perspective. Caroline Robbins, Clinton Rossiter, and Douglass Adair were prominent in dissenting from the orthodox view and in pointing out the non-Lockean roots of the American political tradition.[13] Robbins published a 1947 article in the *William and Mary Quarterly* that in hindsight was the opening shot.[14] In her later book, *The Eighteenth Century Commonwealthman*, Robbins persuasively argued for the importance of the English libertarian heritage to colonial and revolutionary Americans. Men such as Harrington, Milton, Sidney, Neville, Molesworth, and Trenchard and Gordon, she argued, had a central and continuing influence on early American political thought. Douglass Adair documented the impact of David Hume on James Madison's theory of the extended republic, and Clinton Rossiter took a more sympathetic look at the American founders as theorists as well as edging away from Locke's dominance.

Simultaneously, the simple economic determinism that underlay discussions of American political thought in the 1940s was being discredited by both Robert E. Brown and Forrest McDonald.[15] Beard's death in 1948 perhaps symbolized the end of the dominance of progressive historians, but it did not immediately result in a more political and theoretical discussion. Instead, there developed another dominant view that is now termed neoconservative or "consensus" history; Richard Hofstadter, Daniel J. Boorstin, and Louis Hartz were prominent figures in this 1950s' development.[16]

Hofstadter saw a strong continuity in American political

thought but argued that it began in 1787 since the founders in his eyes designed original institutions without reference to earlier events, and this continuity was based on the wholesale adoption of Locke's political principles. Boorstin did not see continuity in American political thought as grounded in Locke but in American circumstance and experience. This "genius of American politics" explains the continuity, the relative lack of conflict, and the absence of ideology in American political history; it also suggests that there is no American political *theory*, or very little, and even that turns out to be neither significant nor original. Louis Hartz, of course, continued to inject the dominance-of-Locke perspective despite the growing doubts about this thesis.

Political scientists went through a similar evolution but for reasons related to changes in their own discipline, not as a result of reading historians. American political science had begun its development toward an empirically oriented social science with the publication of Arthur F. Bentley's *The Process of Government* in 1908.[17] Like the historians, Bentley and the political scientists of his era were deeply influenced by progressivism; indeed Charles Beard and Arthur Bentley were the most prominent members of the "realist school." Unlike Beard, however, Bentley continued to support American exceptionalism insofar as he viewed the United States as an essentially classless society that had escaped the economic stratification of Europe because of its republican government and its wide economic opportunity. His interest-group analysis was the harbinger of contemporary mainstream political science, with its emphasis on political processes rather than on institutions, its pluralist stance as opposed to Beard's class analysis, and its emphasis on the empirical study of contemporary political phenomena divorced from any analysis of values or of the normative, which he termed "ghosts." If he went back to the founding period at all it was to find pluralist political theory in the Madisonian model rather than a design with a theoretical grounding and purpose. For Bentley, American political theory consisted in the development of empirical theory to explain behavioral regularities in the present.[18]

Bentley's pluralist approach was pushed to the center of the discipline by Charles E. Merriam; his *History of American Political Theories* published in 1903 did not shrink from reviewing the entire history of American political theory from the Puritans onward and seeing in it the continuous march of democratic progress. In this sense Merriam, like the progressive historians, saw the past mainly in terms of explaining the present instead of as an era that had to be recaptured in its own different terms. In 1921 Merriam published an influential article that, like Turner's famous lecture on the role of the frontier, defined an emerging research agenda for the future. Merriam argued for a political science that would emphasize method, that would be oriented toward the discovery of political laws that could be used to control public policy, and that would be sustained by organized professional structures to promote research.[19]

As political scientists pursued an increasingly empirical agenda, their findings undercut the progressive assumption of American exceptionalism, and the increasing tension between these two legacies finally reached a breaking point by the late 1940s, most notably in Joseph A. Schumpeter's widely read *Capitalism, Socialism, and Democracy*.[20] Schumpeter still defended the pluralist approach begun by Bentley but argued for the concept that has come to be known as plural elitism. America was not an exception in human history, but because of its democratic institutions the United States had managed to fragment the elite into competing factions and thus avoid the worst effects of elitist dominance. In effect, the pluralist approach was used to overlay a class analysis. Schumpeter's analysis and categories became part of the core theory assumed by mainstream political science. His work was a contribution to American political theory in its own right, but typical of modern political science it was free-floating and did not require, indeed it eschewed, an examination of earlier American political theory since that earlier theory was not "realistic." It is interesting, therefore, that Robert A. Dahl, the most famous and influential exponent of both pluralism and the application of empirical methods to the study of politics, should in 1956 write perhaps the most widely and persistently read book ever written by a political scientist, *A Preface to Democratic Theory*, in which he begins by returning to an analysis of the Madisonian model.[21]

Robert Dahl also published a famous empirical study of New Haven politics, in which he essentially confirmed and refined Schumpeter's model of democratic elitism. Dahl wrote many books and articles in defense of pluralist analysis and was one of the most prominent exponents for a behaviorally oriented discipline. Yet in 1956 he developed a propositional analysis of Madison's theory in *The Federalist* that had an unexpected effect; even though Dahl dismissed Madison's theory as flawed, Dahl's analysis showed to a wide audience the possibility of pursuing American political theory as theory and not simply as ideology. Martin Diamond in 1959 published a rejoinder to Dahl's analysis that was itself widely read and highly influential and that also emphasized the theoretical content of *The Federalist*.[22] Robert Dahl inadvertently set off renewed interest in American political theory from the founding era, and Martin Diamond ensured that *The Federalist* would continue to be taken seriously as theory. Dissertations on the Madisonian model and on political thinkers of eighteenth-century America became a growth industry during the 1960s and 1970s, and the Bicentennial guaranteed that this renewed interest in American political theory would continue into the 1980s.

Another consequence of Dahl's book, especially juxtaposed with Diamond's critique of Dahl, a critique that many scholars think was successful if not devastating, was to separate this renewed interest in American political theory from empirical analysis. Mainstream political science was given a prominent model showing that American political theory could be taken seriously while American political theory focused overwhelmingly on the founding period that Dahl said rested upon a flawed theory. At the very least the protopluralist theory that he found had been superseded by more recent thinking and research and thus could be largely ignored. That the renewed interest in American political theory of the founding period was grounded at least in part upon an effective critique of Dahl's analysis served only to deepen the split between American political theory and mainstream political science. Yet, as I have argued, this split is based upon a misapprehension, one that we now see grows from an intramural battle of the 1950s. Further, American political theory is inherently empirical since it rests upon the analysis of experience. In any case, the end of the 1950s saw political scientists reengaging in political theory but in a way that initially separated it from the mainstream of the discipline.

Meanwhile, the historians were in the process of undergoing

their own drastic revisions. First, the "consensus" school in history was beginning to give way to an emphasis upon discontinuities in American history or else to a more evolutionary view that stressed change. Second, the perspective that saw Locke as dominant was replaced by the view that one version or another of republicanism was dominant during the founding era; J.G.A. Pocock, Bernard Bailyn, and Gordon S. Wood were major figures in this shift.[23] Pocock argued that American political thought was an eighteenth-century extension of classical republican theory, with its emphasis on virtue and the common good. Machiavelli and a host of Renaissance thinkers, it was argued, codified classical republicanism into "civic humanism"; these classical ideals, in their Renaissance synthesis, were passed on to the Americans, said Pocock, through the republican writings of Milton, Harrington, Nedham, Bolingbroke, and Trenchard and Gordon. Pocock decisively broke the tendency to view Locke as dominant, but he still viewed American political thought as essentially ideological rather than theoretical and as derivative of English thought, although now a different version of English ideology, one that in Pocock's view was born in a dread of modernity.

Bernard Bailyn identified five major sources from which colonists drew their political thinking—the writings of classical antiquity, the writings of Enlightenment rationalism, the English common-law tradition, the political and social theories of New England Puritanism (especially covenant theory), and the writers earlier identified by Caroline Robbins as being associated with the English Civil War and the Commonwealth. According to Bailyn, this last group, the radical English Whigs, generated the perspective that brought order and synthesis to the other strands of writing and more than any other source shaped the mind of the American revolutionary generation. Thanks to Bailyn we now had an inclusive, sophisticated synthesis; Pocock's classical writers, Robbins's Commonwealthmen, and some indigenous American Puritan thought were all part of the mix. Locke was also in the mix, although the irony of his position in the blend went unremarked by reviewers of Bailyn's book. Bailyn places Locke among Enlightenment thinkers, but this is surely anachronistic. Members of the founding generation were much more likely to link John Locke with the great English Whig thinker Algernon Sidney, to use their names together in a mantra of equivalence, which makes Locke a prominent member of the very group, the radical English Whigs, that Bailyn says shaped the mind of the Revolutionary War generation.

The new "orthodoxy" defined by Bailyn's synthesis is a slippery paradigm to apply. First, those men who wrote the Declaration of Independence and who ran the Revolution had different needs from those who wrote and adopted the Constitution; a simple citation count has already established that different European writers in different combinations were used during the 1770s, compared with the 1780s.[24] Nor is it always clear where to place individual thinkers: The contemporary scholar Garry Wills places David Hume within the Scottish Enlightenment, Lundberg and May consider him a member of the more radical second Enlightenment, Bailyn does not place him clearly in any category, and many of the founding generation considered Hume a Tory.[25] Without agreement on a stable set of categories and the secure placement of major writers such as Locke and Hume within them, analysis of the relative influence of such traditions remains problematic.

Criticism of Bailyn's republican school has led to a modest resurgence of the theory of Locke's dominance, mostly by those trained in political philosophy, but the single-theorist approach to American political theory is no longer sustainable after Bailyn's analysis, regardless of which category is most suitable for Locke or Hume and no matter which category of thinkers was most influential on the American founding generation.[26] Still, although the theses of Locke's dominance and of economic determinism of the 1940s have finally been discarded by most historians and political scientists, the tendency prevails to look to Europe for an American political theory that seems not to be found in America and to view the appropriated European thought as an ideology rather than as a theory. It is in the context of this tendency that Gordon Wood's work is especially interesting.

The Rediscovery of the Political Class

The impact of Gordon Wood's book, *The Creation of the American Republic*, was immediate and lasting; published more than twenty years ago, it remains fresh and convincing. Still, historians have tended to misperceive Wood's book as simply one of the key works that established the central importance of republican theory for American political thought. A more careful reading shows that Wood's work develops a picture of the American founding that is quite at odds with the classical republican school represented by Pocock, and the difference is crucial for American political theory.

Pocock sees Americans as the ultimate beneficiaries of a classical republicanism recodified by Machiavelli, but Wood carefully reconstructs the evolution of American political thinking that resulted in a distinctively American republican theory—one that was not simply appropriated from European origins. Perhaps even more important, Wood's book brought to fruition a new approach to the study of American political thought, an approach that had quietly emerged in the work of historians and mainstream political scientists but had been largely missed by students of the American founding in political science departments. Gordon Wood showed us how to analyze American political theory by using the works of those writers in the political class rather than the works of those relatively few writers among the elite. To illustrate the importance of Wood's book, we need to return briefly to a discussion of assembled texts.

We can identify three broad tendencies in the assemblage of texts in American political theory. The first and oldest tendency is to examine the writings of the elite; under a presumption that history is guided by and results from the actions of great men, any attempt to explain historical events would seem to require that we look at their writings. The collected papers of Thomas Jefferson, James Madison, George Washington, John Adams, Benjamin Franklin, Alexander Hamilton, and maybe a dozen others would appear to constitute the prime assembled text in American political theory. A further presumption that these men operated within a symbolic environment defined and dominated by other great minds leads to our first assembled text including the works of major European thinkers, those writers with even greater minds, in the context of whose work American elites thought and created. The elitist assumption thus tends to lead us back to one or a few European thinkers such as Locke, Hobbes, Machiavelli, Montesquieu, Hume, or Rousseau.

A concomitant feature of the elitist approach is that we assume the major public documents in American political theory, the Declaration of Independence, the U.S. Constitution, and the U.S. Bill of Rights, were the products of this elite. Those using this methodology openly resist suggestions that Jefferson was merely summarizing the generally held ideas of Americans in the Declaration; or that James Madison, far from being the father of the Constitution, was on the losing side of a majority of the votes taken at the Constitutional Convention and on almost all of the votes that were most important to him; or that the Bill of Rights simply summarized the least common denominator found in state bills of rights written by large numbers of nonelites.[27] These claims may or may not be correct, but those using the elitist approach to assembling texts in American political theory are often uninterested in the actual historical record. The strengths of the elitist position lie in its emphasis on the meaning of history as opposed to a mere recitation of facts, its capacity to generate theories of history that are important and interesting, and its power to remind us that ideas do have consequences. On the negative side, the elitist approach is not, strictly speaking, historical, it is subject to ideological distortion, and it can too often lead to the kind of sterile debate that inclines people to put its practitioners, such as historians of ideas and political philosophers, on the margins of intellectual discourse.

A second and more recent historical development relevant to American political theory is the rise of social history. Essentially, social history attempts to reconstruct the lives of the many people who are without an explicit historical voice, and one could safely characterize such history as democratic in its perspective. Earlier historians were not so much antidemocratic as they were limited by the lack of data, the expense of collecting needed information, and the lack of relevant methodologies. An old observation in the social sciences holds that research tends to use the most readily available information. Social historians have been extremely inventive in their search for surrogate measures of everyday life in earlier historical eras, and they have worked diligently to gather, organize, and analyze their data. The information they have used includes probate-court records, voting data, newspaper circulation patterns, census figures, financial and economic data, mortality statistics, court records, minutes of town meetings, county health records, oral histories, autobiographies, diaries, newspaper ads, political campaign material, and just about any material that can be systematically analyzed. That is, the assembled text used by social historians includes far more than political writings, as these researchers attempt to give a voice to the many. We have learned much and undoubtedly will learn a great deal more about how various nonelite ethnic, racial, occupational, gender, religious, and regional groups lived and what they contributed culturally, socially, and economically; but social history has thus far had relatively little to tell us about American political theory.

Primarily, because of the nature of the data we usually cannot discern the actual thoughts of the people, and when we can the thinking we encounter is at best ideological and not theoretical. We can find patterns in the political behavior of the many, but if no one can tell us the thinking behind the nonvoting of today with any certainty, how are we to recover the theoretical thinking that underlay the voting behavior in the 1700s, assuming the behavior was so informed? In effect, social historians must proceed as other social scientists do; they must theorize about the implications of the information they have systematically uncovered.

A third approach to the history of the American founding has been to examine the writing of those people in what might be termed the political class, and this approach has begun to revolutionize the study of American political theory. The development has gone almost unnoticed by scholars in history and political science alike, but the potential significance for future research is so great that we must take the time to consider the implications and to understand clearly the meaning of the "political class."

Using a variety of methodologies and research settings, mainstream political science has for many years consistently discovered the presence of a subset within the population that disproportionately affects public policy and political outcomes. In nondemocratic systems this subset does not include many people beyond the narrow class of elites, but in systems using elections and other participatory means of popular control this subset, the politically active class, typically includes between 15 and 20 percent of the adult population.[28]

From this political class are drawn most of those people who consistently vote in every election, almost all of those who contribute to election campaigns, and virtually all of those who work for political parties, run for office, work for candidates whether partisan or nonpartisan, organize and work for political-interest groups, write letters to newspapers and government officials, testify before governmental bodies, and write political essays for public consumption.[29] These are the opinion leaders who immerse themselves in information about issues, candidates, and policies, and therefore the rest of the population looks to them for cues when deciding how to think about political matters, what opinions to hold, and how to vote.

These opinion leaders do not control the political opinions and actions of those people in the less active political orders but rather process the information for them, present the alternatives, and provide important cues. In fact, many or most people not in the political class use certain members of the political class as negative cue givers. That is, most people learn to identify those leaders with whom they do not agree as well as those with whom they agree and use cues provided by both types of opinion makers in sorting out their own views. For instance, a citizen who harbors negative attitudes toward those individuals who oppose the war in Vietnam might see a number of bumper stickers against the war paired with bumper stickers opposed to nuclear power. Finding cues in favor of nuclear power from those opinion makers among the political class this citizen admires, the person might significantly alter his or her attitude toward nuclear power to a positive one.

Those scholars who use rationality models to analyze human behavior would point to this division of labor between the cue-giving politically active class and those people who are less active as an example of cost-minimizing rationality, whereby the less aware and active citizens get a relatively free ride upon the hard work and information-gathering of the political class.

In the context of the American founding, the political class would express itself most clearly either through popularly approved documents of political foundation such as the Declaration of Independence, the various state constitutions, and the U.S. Constitution or through public political statements such as petitions to legislators, newspaper essays, books, and published pamphlets. Other forms of political participation, such as demonstrations, speeches, and informal political discussions, would not survive to the present, although speeches were often reprinted in pamphlet form. In sum, these public documents would have been written by members of the active political class and would together allow us to study the intentions, motivations, and theoretical reasoning of this political class. Before such an approach to American political theory could be used, however, these materials first had to be made available for study, and then their use had to be sanctioned as appropriate in place of or in addition to the writings of the political elite.

In the middle 1960s just such material began to be published, almost simultaneously, by a number of scholars in both history and political science. Prominent among the former, Bernard Bailyn published his collection of political pamphlets in 1965 and immediately caught the attention of both disciplines. In the same year Morton Borden published an edited version of the Antifederalist papers, and the following year Cecelia Kenyon published her collection of Antifederalist pamphlets. The definitive edition of *The Federalist*, which was originally a series of newspaper essays, had been published by Jacob E. Cooke in 1961. Also in 1965 Frederick Rudolph published his collection of pamphlets and essays from the founding era on theories of education. In 1966 Oscar and Mary Handlin published a large collection of materials, including pamphlets, essays, town convention records, and referenda returns surrounding the rejected Massachusetts constitution of 1778. Also in 1966, Leonard Levy published a large collection of eighteenth-century public documents and essays relating to freedom of the press in America.[30]

Nor were the historians alone, although political scientists came late to the task. In 1967 Charles S. Hyneman and George W. Carey reprinted portions of the debates from the first session of the U.S. Congress, and Herbert J. Storing published an article in 1976 that provided a complete list of pamphlets written in support of the proposed U.S. Constitution. Then Herbert Storing, with the assistance of Murray Dry, published a seven-volume collection of pamphlets, *The Complete Antifederalist*, in 1981; and Charles Hyneman and Donald S. Lutz published their two volume *American Political Writing during the Founding Era: 1760–1805* in 1983. Together these two collections doubled the number of easily accessible political pamphlets from the founding era. Finally, in 1986 Philip B.

Kurland and Ralph Lerner published their five-volume collection, *The Founders' Constitution*, which contained pamphlets, newspaper articles, and letters and public documents, among other writings. By this time more than five hundred political pamphlets and hundreds of other documents or essays had been reprinted, and hundreds more had been identified for easy access by scholars.[31]

This outpouring of reprinted materials from the founding era has had a profound effect on the study of American political theory. First, these collections provided texts, assembled texts, that allowed us to approach the political theory of the founding more systematically and more comprehensively. Second, this material changed our view of the intellectual currents at work during the American founding, broadened our perspective, and led to a reading of a much wider range of European political thinkers. Third, the availability of this material refocused our attention on political theory as it existed on this side of the Atlantic, including colonial antecedents. Fourth, we began to take our own political documents seriously again as texts that could be analyzed for theoretical content, including state documents. Fifth, the material led to the rediscovery of a political class that included but spread well beyond the relatively few well-known men of the late eighteenth century.

Early in this process of rediscovery Gordon Wood published a book embodying these changes in our view of the founding that represented a synthesis of considerable importance. Wood's magisterial work, published in 1969, was grounded squarely in the writings of the political class of the founding era. Not only did he draw upon the writings of the political class, he quoted generously from their contents so that fully one-fifth of his six-hundred-page book is composed of passages from these writings. Wood apparently worked assiduously to find precisely the right quote that conveyed either the typical sentiment or a nuance in some variant opinion. More important, perhaps, is the unstated use of these writings as equivalent to a social science data base upon which to securely ground his analysis; his use of the pamphlet literature constituted a claim that anyone who examined the same literature would reach the same or similar conclusions. In effect, Wood carefully sampled a data base upon which to rest his analysis and conclusions. The list of ninety-six pamphlets at the end of Wood's *Creation of the American Republic* and the state and national

constitutional documents around which they were written were together an assembled text, a carefully constructed sampling of a
broader data base comprising all documents and publications generated by the political class. Gordon Wood's work indicated clearly
the direction for future historical research on American political
theory.

A focus on the political class is an improvement in several respects; for one thing, it allows us to place the writings by political
elites within a realistic, political context that helps us understand
those writings. Since its original settling, America has encouraged
people of genius to compete as members of a broadly defined political class, a class that absorbs, considers, argues about, modifies,
and then transmits to other portions of the public a refined, reduced, yet still competitive set of reasons for acting together in one
fashion or another. That is, the political class includes the elites but
forces the elites to operate within a much broader set of the population than was the case before the United States initiated its "new
order for the ages." The relationship of the elites to the broader political class is complex and bilateral. We study the writings of the
political class to discover the manner and extent to which elite
ideas penetrate and are accepted as well as not accepted. For example, we may find that some individuals among the elite, such as
Hamilton, wanted an elective monarchy but that this idea had no
chance of being accepted by the broad political class that dominated the constitution-making process. We also study the writings
of the political class to discover the extent to which members of the
elite summarize and synthesize the ideas widely held within the
political class. The genius of a great political leader, after all, often
lies not in the creation of new ideas but in the capture and dramatic
codification of widely held but still pretheoretical ideas, for example, Thomas Jefferson's brilliant summary and codification of what
he called "the American mind" in the Declaration of Independence.[32] In sum, studying the writings of the broader political class
not only includes the writings of the elite but puts those elite writings in context and greatly helps us to understand their meaning.

Also, a focus upon the political class helps us understand the
behavior, and to a certain extent the thinking, of those people in
the broader, nonactivist population. The political class in a political
system based upon popular consent serves on the one hand as the

cue-giver for mass political behavior—as the part of the population that defines issues, works up competing responses to problems, and argues about the reasons for taking one course of action over another. To the extent that the political class performs the function of downward transmission, its ideas structure more general public opinion and political behavior.

On the other hand, many or most people in the political class, dependent upon support from the nonactivist population to carry out their political agendas, seek to understand and project upward the opinions, needs, interests, and ideas of the various members of the nonactivist population. To the extent that the political class performs the function of upward transmission, it becomes our best window into the general population and the best way to understand broader political phenomena. Thus, the material that the social historians uncover—as well as the findings of political scientists focusing on mass behavior like electoral politics, public opinion, and political culture—becomes more accessible through the study of the political class. This insight becomes not so much grounds for dismissing mass behavior as manipulated by the political class but grounds for asking how successful the political class has been in its bidirectional function of transmission and for questioning the extent to which the political class may be engaged in manipulating the broader population rather than in interpreting their views.

A focus on the political class also results in an improvement in methodology. Consider the tendency in the past to base the study of American political theory on the writings of a relatively few elites. The elitist approach, regardless of its intention, can be viewed as a solution to a sampling problem raised by an attempted causal analysis. Using the U.S. Constitution as an example, the elitists were proposing a cause that would explain the content of the Constitution, the significance or meaning of that content for its readers, and the structured political activity that would result from that meaning. The content, meaning, and resulting behavior are, in effect, the dependent variables in the causal analysis. As the independent variable the elitists propose human intention codified in a theory. In other words, ideas have consequences, and one possible consequence is the structuring of human political behavior through a constitution that embodies a deductively linked set of ideas called a theory. The theory describes the expected pattern of behavior, explains why it is to be expected, why it is to be preferred, and how the provisions of the Constitution function to produce these results. To this point we have rehearsed the assumptions underlying any constitutional theory.

The difficulty with the elitist approach is that it oversimplifies the causal analysis by giving a privileged status to the writings of a very few individuals. That is, the elitists both undersample and skew their sample; they undersample those writers relevant for producing political outcomes and skew their sample by using enduring reputation or fame as the basis for inclusion in the sample. This practice of undersampling requires a bit of elaboration. If the theory underlying a constitution is to produce the intended pattern of human activity, those people who read the document must basically agree on its requirements. Even assuming that a few individuals created the theory on their own, a position that cannot be empirically sustained, unless those people who read the document understand its intentions and the reasoning that justifies the pattern of behavior the constitution is designed to produce, the people who are to be bound by the constitution must either be forced to live by its contents, which is contrary to the rule of consent upon which constitutionalism rests, or else the people must be manipulated or hoodwinked into accepting the document, which is also contrary to that rule.

In the ancient world a constitution was handed to a people by a Solon, a Draco, or a Hammurabi; in modern constitutionalism, under an assumption of popular sovereignty, the people are not "handed" anything. The intentions of the few do not constitute the independent variable. Rather, the independent variable, the political theory and ideas behind a constitution, is the result of a self-conscious, reflexive, complicated political process that involves enough people so that the intent of the constitution can be transmitted downward, just as the preferences of the people can be transmitted upward. Without the political process, and the political class that is at its center, the elite would lack both the information and the resources to force, hoodwink, persuade, or mollify anyone. The political class is too large to be represented by a sample of writing from five or six or even ten people, and naturally there will never be enough famous people to constitute any kind of reasonable sample of a political class. Nor is fame necessarily a good basis for selecting a sample of people relevant to political theory. George Washington was, and continues to be, the most famous person from the founding era, but few people will argue that Washington has a special importance for the creation of American political theory.

Why, then, has there been a tendency to use the writings of a few elites as the basis for American political theory? The best reason may be that until recently their writings were readily available because of their fame; the writings of the nonfamous were not. With the availability of a much larger sample of writing from the political class, the elite can now be read in a broader context, and because of the nature of constitutionalism and the position of the political class in a constitutional system, the writings of the elite must be placed within that broader context.

A further methodological advantage derived from focusing upon the political class is that in doing so we are pushed away from the "exchange of paradigms" approach that distorts more than it illuminates American political theory. As Gordon S. Wood has suggested in a recent review, historians often construct categories for use in organizing a complicated reality, but the debate over whether the founders were Lockean liberals, classical republicans, or children of the Enlightenment results from asking the wrong question.

> The question of which tradition in the late eighteenth century was more dominant—republicanism or liberalism—is badly posed. It assumes a sharp dichotomy between two clearly identifiable traditions that eighteenth century reality will not support. None of the historical participants, including the Founding Fathers, ever had any sense that he had to choose between republicanism and liberalism, between Machiavelli and Locke.[33]

The founders could hold simultaneously and without any sense of inconsistency principles from several theoretical traditions. Although these principles might appear contradictory from the viewpoint of European political theory, the political reality inhabited by Americans made the principles perfectly compatible.

For example, at the Constitutional Convention the competing views of the English constitution represented by Montesquieu's separation-of-powers perspective, Blackstone's mixed-government approach, and Hume's balanced-faction analysis, though mutually incompatible in the English context, were included in the Constitution that emerged from the convention's deliberations.[34]

Contrary to the tendency of recent scholars of either the "liberal" or the "republican" schools anachronistically to invent paradigms into which political writings of the founding era are forced, American political theory needs to be studied in terms of the categories used by those engaged in developing it.[35] Nor is this approach simply a methodological nicety. American political theory is distinguished from European political theory precisely because it rests upon the work of the political class and not on the writings of an intellectual elite. Any attempt to derive American political theory primarily from the writings of European intellectuals or to describe American political theory as dominated by an intellectual tradition is fundamentally to misconstrue the enterprise. The entire point of American political theory from the beginning was to replace elite dominance with popular control, to ground politics directly in human experience rather than in philosophical utopias, and to codify theoretically the ideas and behavior patterns that emerged from the political process rather than to force the political process into conformity with an abstraction. The rediscovery of the political class is a recovery of American political theory as it was created. As Gordon Wood points out when discussing the emergence of the doctrine of popular sovereignty:

> These were revolutionary ideas that had unfolded rapidly in the decade after Independence, but not deliberately or evenly. Men were always only half aware of where their thought was going, for these new ideas about politics were not the products of extended reasoned analysis but were rather numerous responses of different Americans to a swiftly changing reality, of men involved in endless polemics compelled to contort and draw out from the prevailing assumptions the latent logic few had foreseen. Rarely before 1787 were these new thoughts comprehended by anyone as a whole. They were bits and pieces thrown up by the necessities of argument and condi-

tion, without broad design or significance. But if crystalized by sufficient pressures they could result in a mosaic of an entirely new conception of politics to those who would attempt to describe it.[36]

European political theory is codified in books written by men who essentially stood outside the political process, observed it, and then developed theories for explaining what they saw and what they wanted; American political theory has proceeded differently. Until recently, and certainly during the founding era, political theory was not written by detached, philosophical observers or by academic political theorists but by those engaged more immediately in politics. Under conditions of liberty that permitted anyone who wished to enter the politically active class, the widely shared assumptions of those people in the political class led to behavior, hopes, and conflicts that required more explicit codification if the political class was to be mobilized in a coherent and effective manner. The codification emerged from the evolving reasoned analysis used to mobilize this class and at some point became widely accepted theory. That is, theory in America followed evolving practice in a manner analogous to the way in which anthropologists tell us that myth follows ritual. Some members of the political class saw further and more quickly and thus had a much greater impact on the codification of theory as well as on extending its implications. These great minds had to work within the shared assumptions and accepted institutional practices of the political class, and any theoretical innovations they produced eventually had to be ratified and supported by the political class, but there was considerable room for leadership. Nor were these political leaders devoid of theoretical ideas outside of the political process to draw upon; they could use any ideas or explanations from European political theory as long as these fit within the envelope of possibilities defined by the assumptions and practices shared by the political class. But the political class would not tolerate a wholesale imposition of a political theory from abroad that did not fit into their presuppositions and that was not based upon their consent. Thus, an understanding of American political theory, as long as it continues to emerge from and is ratified by the political class, will require us to use history, especially that of the political class.

Gordon Wood calls this dynamic relationship between political leaders and the broader political class "an elitist theory of democracy" and attributes it to the Federalists as distinguished from the American Whigs of the revolutionary years.[37] But his general analysis of American politics during the 1770s and 1780s is consistent with a model in which a political class mediates between the elites and the general population with both an upward and a downward function of communication; in which elections are used to choose among policy options, candidates, and theoretical codifications that are worked out in the political class; and in which a fractured or plural elite competes for the support of the political class and thus ultimately for the support of the broader population. With the rediscovery of the political class by historians comes a fundamental convergence between historical analysis and empirical political science.

Although it is true that Americans are not now and never were intellectual stand-ins for European political thinkers, it is also true that Americans have used and greatly benefited from European political philosophy. To say that no one European can be credited with a decisive or a dominant influence on American political theory does not imply the absence of important influences. The point I am arguing here is threefold. First, no one European thinker dominated because Americans read and drew upon many European thinkers. Second, no European intellectual tradition dominated because those philosophers to whom Americans turned were spread over several "traditions," and the supposed traditions were themselves mixed, interpenetrating each other, so that individual thinkers can often be simultaneously assigned to several traditions. Third, it is still an open question as to where Americans found many of the ideas they borrowed to help in the construction of the melange called American political theory. It is necessary for those in the discipline to "sample" the European literature more carefully, and before sampling can occur we need to identify the intellectual universe, a task to which we now turn.

Chapter 5

Intellectual History and the American Founding

Part of the preface to American political theory includes the history of how it has been studied in the past, which sheds light on our current status in the enterprise and how we got here. From such a review a number of lessons can be drawn on how not to proceed, including a stricture against the use of intellectual "traditions" to explain the genesis of American political theory. Therefore, it might strike some as perverse that immediately after such strong cautions I am embarking on a discussion of those intellectual traditions.

Although it is perfectly reasonable to conclude that European thinkers were read by the founding generation and influenced American political thinking, it is important to understand who was read and how. I hope that the discussion will open up the entire range of European writers relevant to American political theory for future research and have included as an appendix a comprehensive list of secular authors available to Americans of the middle and late eighteenth century (see pp. 159–64). These authors and their works are more or less sorted into "traditions" in this chapter, both from our point of view and from that of the founding generation. The point of such a sorting is to suggest who might be read as representative of a particular approach, thus providing the reader with an initial entrée into a literature that is largely unknown today. One result of the discussion is to see an increase in the number of intellectual "traditions" that we must consider relevant; another is to reinforce the previous conclusion that because many major figures are difficult to place and because some traditions have problematic definitional boundaries, the utility of intellectual

113

traditions for describing and explaining American political theory is severely limited. Finally, just as these European writers stand as part of the preface to the political theory of the founding, the way in which the founders appropriated European thinking stands as a preface to how American political theory has continued to use European sources. That is, Americans appropriated theory from overseas in accord with their own needs as informed by their own experience. Once we understand better the process of such intellectual appropriation during the founding, the better we will understand American use of European ideas down to this day.

If American political theory is to become a discipline, those engaged in it must use a greater range of texts and must be more systematic in their use. This means reading more widely in the public documents, pamphlets, and other writings by Americans in the political class as well as gaining a wider familiarity with European thinkers. As a minor example of the insight we gain by doing so, consider the version of John Locke's "life, liberty, and property" that Jefferson put in the Declaration of Independence—"life, liberty, and the pursuit of happiness." Greater familiarity with the American pamphlet literature would show that Jefferson's formulation had already appeared in the writings of John Adams, James Wilson, Alexander Hamilton, George Mason, James Otis, and Richard Bland, to name a few, and that it did not originate with Jefferson. More important, a wider familiarity with European thinkers would show prior use of the formulation of happiness as an end of government by William Wollaston, Cesare Beccaria, Jean Jacques Burlamaqui, and Henry St. John Bolingbroke—including discussion of the meaning of the term and why it is part of government's job. Since all four of these men were widely read by Americans of the founding generation, exactly how and why the formulation was appropriated becomes an interesting and possibly an important question.[1]

This diverse European literature, and the manner in which Americans used it, is an important part of the material that students of American political theory ought to know before conducting their own inquiries. The discussion that follows is an attempt to unravel and identify the various intellectual strands used by the founders to weave American political thought during the eighteenth century. Perhaps a better metaphor is the peeling back of layers, as with an onion; there we shall find the place to begin—underlying the several skins, giving them shape, is the concept that Americans of the eighteenth century called "experience."

Experience Must Be Our Guide

At the end of *The Federalist*, Hamilton quotes David Hume. "The judgments of many must unite in the work; EXPERIENCE must guide their labour; TIME must bring it to perfection; and the FEELING of inconveniences must correct the mistakes which they *inevitably* fall into in their first trials and experiments."[2] This statement serves as a succinct introduction to the most fundamental aspect of both Federalist and Antifederalist thought, namely, the conviction that as useful as books can be, politics should always rest upon a base of human experience rather than upon logical abstractions, no matter how appealing or moral the abstractions. Americans based their state constitutions upon their colonial institutions, and their colonial institutions had evolved from the basis of the colonists' own experiences in shaping them to meet their needs. The Federalists had in turn built upon the state constitutions as well as on the Articles of Confederation.

Their colonial ancestors had been largely practical, rather than theoretical, in their policy, although the Bible had provided them with a coherent basis for thinking about politics. Covenant theology had deeply informed their earliest constitutions, such as the Pilgrim Code of Law (1636) and the Fundamental Orders of Connecticut (1639). Yet secularization gradually had moved the colonists away from direct reliance upon religion to justify their form of government. The essential test was that on a day-to-day basis their institutions worked.

Colonial political institutions were generally established in a single document, a covenant or compact, which functioned as a constitution; indeed, these people invented the modern written constitution. The compact in turn rested upon de facto popular consent, even though no theory of popular sovereignty as yet existed.[3] All political institutions were guided by majority rule or by those elected by a majority. These political practices were considerably different from British precedent. For example, in England property requirements resulted in a distinct minority of adult males being able to vote, and although a majority of those votes produced electoral victory, it was never intended that winners actually represent a majority of the population. In America, because of the availability of cheap land and the absence of an aristocracy and a gentry, the same common-law property requirements enfranchised a majority of adult males, and thus elections expressed something closer to true majority rule. Furthermore, unlike in Britain, it was intended that those elected represent a majority. These practices, then, were of American invention—invention by the many and adjusted over time on the basis of experience.

The first component of experience, then, was the cumulative experience on American shores prior to 1776; the second was the insight that the Federalists had personally and directly gained during their own lives. The drafting of state constitutions and the Articles of Confederation had involved all but a few of them at the Constitutional Convention, and they had felt the consequences of these documents. *The Federalist* is full of explicit and implicit criticism of these earlier documents, not because they were worthless but because the experiences of many of them, over time, had inevitably uncovered mistakes that needed to be corrected.

A third aspect of experience was history. Federalists and Antifederalists alike viewed human history as relevant experience, although certain historical eras were more useful than others.[4] The more religious saw the history of the Jewish people in the Bible as important for understanding republican institutions since it described what they considered to be a Hebraic republic and then showed God's displeasure when the Hebrews replaced their republic with a king. The Roman republic, classical Athens, Italian city-states during the Renaissance, and seventeenth-century Netherlands were viewed as particularly relevant.

Above all, the history of England was ransacked for telling examples. A considerable literature grew up that purported to see the history of England as the story of republican government unfolding. David Hume was most widely read, not for his philosophy but for his *History of England*.[5] Other widely read historians were Bulstrode Whitelock, Paul de Rapin-Thoyras, William Guthrie, Edward Montagu, Oliver Goldsmith, William Temple, James Ralph, Charles Rollin, Jonathan Swift, and Catharine Macaulay.

Americans read these English histories avidly and saw in their own young country the true fulfillment of English promise. The primary connection Americans had with classical Greece and Rome was through their historians. The most widely read Romans were Cicero, Livy, and Tacitus; the Greeks were Polybius, Demosthenes, Thucydides, and Aristotle, although Plutarch's *Lives* was easily the most widely read classical work. *The Federalist*, typical of American political writing in this regard, is filled with historical examples as part of the Federalist dedication to experience as the fount of wisdom.

The Republican Tradition

The historians taught the founders that a republican form of government was best. These historians were not writing history for academic reasons but to justify the creation of republican government, usually in England. One leg of republican theory stood on dissenting Protestantism and thus reinforced the impact of religion on American political thought; the other leg stood on classical political thought, beginning with Aristotle but usually learned from Cicero and the Romans. Machiavelli was important for rediscovering republican thought and translating it for the modern world, but Americans actually became most familiar with republican theory as a result of those thinkers writing in the context of the English civil war.[6]

Unfortunately, there was no consensus on the components of a republican form of government; four definitions from the era illustrate the diversity.

Whenever I use the word *republic* with approbation, I mean a government in which the people have collectively, or by representation, an essential share in sovereignty. (John Adams in a letter to Samuel Adams, October 18, 1790)[7]

Is not the *whole* sovereignty, my friend, essentially in the people? . . . Is it not the uncontrollable, essential right of the people to amend and alter or annul their constitution and frame a new one . . . [have] annual or biennial elections . . . and by empowering their representatives to impeach the greatest officers of the state? (Samuel Adams in a letter to John Adams, November 20, 1790)[8]

a government by its citizens in mass, acting directly, according to rules established by the majority. (Thomas Jefferson in a letter to John Taylor, May 28, 1816)[9]

We may define a republic to be . . . a government which derives all its powers either directly or indirectly from the great body of the people, and is administered by persons holding their offices during pleasure, for a limited period, or during good behavior.[10]

The first definition, by John Adams, represents a traditional Whig position that equates republicanism with representation, although "silent allowance" or tacit consent is part of the definition. This passive element was reflected in the colonies by what is known as "the politics of deference." English Whigs of the Commonwealth period essentially adhered to this position and viewed Parliament, not the people, as sovereign authority in the nation state. The second definition reflects the radical Whig position that predominated among those colonists writing the early state constitutions and conducting the American Revolution. It emphasized popular sovereignty with direct, active consent as the basis for all facets of government—direct in the sense that the people gave it themselves and active in that their consent was required frequently, through means in addition to elections, instead of assuming that consent was given through passive acquiescence.

Jefferson's definition, though not reflecting his actual preference, embodied the tendency that was popular in some parts of America to abandon an emphasis upon representation in favor of a republicanism that stressed what we now call democracy. The more democratic version would take a firmer hold in nineteenth-century America as Jacksonian democracy and then later in the Grange and Populist movements. Madison's definition conveys precisely the Federalist notion. Basing his view upon the idea that popular sovereignty only requires the people to rule in an ultimate sense through their approval of the Constitution, Madison allowed for those in government to be either directly or *indirectly* connected to the people through elections.

The juxtaposition of these definitions nicely summarizes how the Federalists built upon the radical Whigs, utterly rejected pure democracy, and softened the democratic component of radical Whig theory, although not to the extent of returning to traditional Whig parliamentary sovereignty. Since those individuals labeled "Antifederalist" were in fact American Whigs, one can see that the Federalists were building upon what had come before and were not rejecting entirely the position of their opponents, the Antifederalists, who as a group were committed to a range of radical and conservative Whiggism. It was this diversity that allowed the Federalists to position themselves successfully during the ratification debate.

On the one hand the Federalists could claim that they were more conservative than many Whigs since, for example, they had backed off from the more radical demands for a directly elected unitary government; but on the other hand they could claim that they were more radical than many Whigs since, for example, the lower house in the new Constitution was to be directly elected and the legislature under the Articles of Confederation had been elected by the state legislatures. The Federalists could thus portray themselves as moderates for seeking a middle position vis-à-vis the two wings of their opposition—as halfway between the Virginia and New Jersey plans. It is no accident that during the ratification debates the Federalists targeted the middle-of-the-road Antifederalists (or Whigs); therefore it is easy to see how John Adams and others who shared his moderate or centrist Whig views could be persuaded to become Federalists.

American Whigs believed they were the heirs of English Whig theory from the seventeenth-century Commonwealth period in England. Locke and Sidney, who were viewed by eighteenth-century Americans as Commonwealthmen or Whigs, are sometimes looked upon today as part of a tradition we now term "liberalism." That is, many people today read Locke as a defender of limited government, individualism, natural rights, and laissez-faire economics—i.e., government should interfere in the economy only to enforce contracts and to punish crimes. He was undoubtedly a contributor to classical liberalism so defined, but one should be careful not to attribute to him the full-blown, complete liberalism that finally evolved in the late nineteenth century. He was much closer to the republicanism of his age that, although it saw individuals as having natural rights, did not include among these rights the list of limits we now expect in a typical American bill of rights. Rather, republican theory as it was understood in late eighteenth-century America saw government as based upon the consent of the people, with almost all other rights viewed as civil rights and therefore susceptible to alienation by a legislature that was supreme. Republican theorists like Locke also saw few limits on the majority; it took James Madison and later theorists to recognize the dangers of the tyranny of the majority. Thus it makes a great deal of difference that Locke was viewed by Americans of the 1780s as a republican theorist, whether we now agree with their interpretation or not.

Also, remember that the distinction between liberalism and republicanism that we might make today was not made in the eighteenth century, since, among other factors, the words "liberal" and "liberalism" had not yet been used to describe political ideas. "Republic," on the other hand, was very much in use by Americans after 1776, even though "republicanism" as a term to describe the theory supporting a preference for republican government had not yet been coined. Pocock and other historians argue that eighteenth-century republicanism can be traced through the mediation of Machiavelli to the republicanism of the ancients, but eighteenth century American assumptions and arguments in favor of a republic more often than not owed considerably more to the fires of evolving political controversy and to modern political theorists than to ancient Greece and Rome. Linking American preferences for a republic with the views of ancient republican theorists is just one more attempt to attribute American political theory, with its assembled texts and experientially based constitutionalism, to European sources. "Republicanism" and "liberalism" are terms we use today to distinguish categories of earlier thinkers; neither these terms nor the distinctions they imply were part of eighteenth-century America.

Americans thus viewed Sidney and Locke as contributors to the Whig theory of politics, which supported a form of government known in late eighteenth-century America as a republic. Algernon Sidney (1622–1683), a contemporary of Thomas Hobbes (1588–1678) and John Locke (1632–1704), was put to death by the

Royalists for having written *Discourses Concerning Government* in support of a republic over a monarchy, even though the manuscript was not published until 1698, well after Sidney's death. The fact of his execution, plus the radical content of his political tract, made Sidney famous during the era of the Glorious Revolution. In America his and Locke's names were likely to be used together as virtual theoretical brothers, both in support of a republican form of government.

Algernon Sidney and John Locke reached similar conclusions and used similar concepts and terminology, but Locke defended a position closer to the traditional Whig view characterized by John Adams's definition; Sidney was closer to the more radical position defended by Samuel Adams. Furthermore, Sidney derived his conclusions from religious premises, copiously citing the Bible and religious authorities; Locke based his on grounds of rationality, which was more typical of the Enlightenment. Regardless, Americans, including Federalists, were very much republicans in the Whig tradition, and they learned their republicanism by reading Sidney, Locke, the historians, and a host of others.[11] Moreover, as with the historians, the Whigs were read in a way to justify and extend the institutions that Americans had already developed. It is an irony of history that John Locke was used by Americans to justify institutions that Americans had developed before Locke published.

The English Commonwealth tradition, often referred to as Whig political theory, was associated with the attempt by Parliament to gain the upper hand over the crown. A powerful ally in this long struggle with the king was the common-law tradition, which emphasized the role of law as a restraint or limit on the crown. Also associated with the democratic tendencies of English Whig political theory was an evolving view of the world that we now call classical liberalism, even though it was a development of modern political theory that had nothing to do with classical Greece or Rome. Interestingly, Locke is also considered a central figure in this latter movement.[12]

The principles of the movement we now call "liberalism" did more than support Whiggism; eventually, this tendency within Whig political theory came to the fore and changed the Whig view of politics altogether. Among other things, it provided reasons for limiting not only the Crown but government as a whole. In some respects a part of more radical Whig political thought and in some respects of more traditional Whiggism, liberal political assumptions blended with two other, more modern movements, Enlightenment rationalism and scientific empiricism. The Federalists absorbed all of these ideas, as did the Antifederalists, but the Federalists would be distinguished by being more in tune with the Enlightenment, especially the Scottish Enlightenment, and by being much more inclined toward the creation of a science of politics.

Lawyers and Liberals

An important part of the English common-law tradition was its emphasis upon law as a restraint on the power of the Crown. The common-law tradition effectively began with Magna Carta in 1215. In Magna Carta the barons forced King John to submit to a number of limits, the most important of which turned out to be Parliament's control of the purse. Magna Carta was ignored for long stretches of time, but Sir John Fortescue resurrected it with his compilation of the common law in the fifteenth century. Of much greater importance was Chief Justice Sir Edward Coke's *Institutes of the Laws of England* (published in four parts between 1628 and 1644). Coke's Whiggish treatment of the common law became the standard work for more than a century, and those Americans with legal training in the colonies were familiar with Coke, which was not an unmixed blessing. James Madison, Thomas Jefferson, John Adams, James Wilson, and Alexander Hamilton were just a few men who were led to speak at some point in their private writings of their relief that the turgid, almost unreadable volumes by Coke had been effectively replaced in time for their own study by the publication of William Blackstone's *Commentaries on the Laws of England*.

Sir John Davies and Nathaniel Bacon, among others, supported Coke's position that the Crown was limited by an "ancient constitution" composed of custom "beyond the memory of man" and the common law built upon such custom. Supporters of the Crown attacked this notion, but a large number of legal historians supported Coke.[13] Finally, between 1765 and 1769 Sir William Blackstone published his four-volume *Commentaries on the Laws of England*. Blackstone's work represented an important fusion in intellectual history. On the one hand, he summarized and extended the common-law position of Coke and his supporters among the legal historians. On the other hand, he synthesized their views with Newton's vision of the universe and Locke's theories of human nature and political liberty. Just as Newton had found the laws underlying physical processes in nature, Blackstone consciously attempted to reveal the fundamental principles underlying British legal and political institutions. Implicit in the principles he found was the Lockean view of rational human nature—the view that all humans are capable of and inclined to engage in careful, reasoned calculations concerning their safety, comfort, and interests. In addition to quoting Locke with some frequency, Blackstone's work is an extension of Locke's ideas.

Locke's *An Essay Concerning Human Understanding*, which contained his view of human nature and psychology, was readily available and widely read in America, but *Two Treatises on Government*, which contained his political theory, was not as widely read there[14]. Locke's direct influence was strongest around the time of the Declaration of Independence, for he wrote profoundly on the reasons for resisting tyranny and on the basis for founding government.[15] Yet he was rarely cited after 1781; instead, Blackstone became the primary, although indirect, means for injecting Locke's ideas into the debate on the Constitution. After Montesquieu, the Federalists cited Blackstone most frequently, followed by Locke, who had relatively little to say about specific institutions or problems of constitutional design. His influence during the constitutional debate resulted from Blackstone's use of Lockean principles to undergird his own institutional analysis. Although Blackstone's interpretation of Locke is sometimes open to question, Blackstone did successfully link the common law with liberal natural-rights theory. Both Federalists and Antifederalists were, in the end, students more of Blackstone than of Locke.

Locke was also present in the background to Federalist thinking through his contributions to liberalism and natural-law theory. Locke had a significant influence on the development of liberalism through his successful synthesis of the concepts of social compact, consent, individualism, and political equality. We do not find an emphasis on any of these concepts in *The Federalist*, although, with the exception of individualism, these concepts are central to American political writing generally. Locke influenced the development of natural-law theory during the eighteenth century through the works of Jean Jacques Burlamaqui and Emmerich de Vattel, although in this regard Locke was a conduit more than an originator since he owed his natural-law view of the state to men like Richard Hooker, Hugo de Grotius, and Baron Samuel von Pufendorf, whom the Federalists and Antifederalists also cited directly.

The assumptions and principles that came to constitute classical liberalism, and John Locke's particular contributions to this movement, thus had a general and indirect effect on the founders through several links—Whig political theory, the common law, natural-law theory, and perhaps most important, the Scottish Enlightenment.

The Scottish Enlightenment

The Scottish Enlightenment did not really derive from the continental Enlightenment but rather from the traditions of republicanism and liberalism, which it blended, adapted, and in important respects altered. The Scottish movement had three basic thrusts—a theory of moral philosophy, a theory of economic progress, and a theory of history. A key figure in its approach to moral philosophy was Francis Hutcheson (1694–1746).

Hutcheson argued, contrary to Locke, that the moral sense of humans was innate rather than the product of reason and that this innate moral sense ultimately inclined people to sociable and public-regarding behavior. Hutcheson saw self-love as the fundamental force in human nature, much as Newton saw gravity as a fundamental force in nature—self-love defined as the natural desire to establish one's superior worth. Self-love had two positive effects on human behavior: First, it led to industriousness, and second, it led people to be industrious in ways that produced social approval. Industriousness had its primary outlet in economic activity, and increasing the common wealth was the very definition of political virtue—seeking the common good. One critical political aspect lay in the seeking of fame. Why would an individual neglect his or her economic betterment to work for the common good? Hutcheson's answer was that the highest social approval to be gained, the most enduring source of fame, resulted from the industrious seeking of the common good through the holding of political office. The seeking of fame, a form of self-love, bestirred a person to work for the common good. Self-love, a kind of self-interest, was thus compatible with virtue defined as pursuit of the common good; indeed, it was seen as the basis of virtue. Humans, when left alone to pursue their interests freely, were naturally cooperative, sociable, benevolent, and virtuous.

One can see that Hutcheson's emphasis on sociableness resonated with the communitarianism that formed the core of American experience from colonial times as well as with the Calvinist emphasis on virtues like industry, frugality, and temperance. Yet even though Hutcheson saw the moral sense as implanted by God, his theory of moral sentiments, of the supremacy of sentiment or innate sense over reason in moral decisions, opened the door to a completely secular analysis of human virtue and human behavior—a secular analysis that was motivated by the desire to develop a science of human behavior derived from fundamental principles similar to Newton's work in physics. An important and thus far unresolved question, then, is to what extent did Publius and other authors of the founding era write from a rationalist perspective derived from liberals like Locke, and to what extent did they write from a theory of moral sentiments. The evidence in *The Federalist* seems to run in both directions, as, with some notable exceptions in New England, it did in American political writing generally.

Recent studies have begun to emphasize the importance of the Scottish Enlightenment for early American political theory in general and for *The Federalist* in particular.[16] Other names associated with Hutcheson are David Hume, Henry Home (Lord Kames), Adam Smith, Thomas Reid, Hugh Blair, and James Beattie. Among these, Hume had the the most immediate and important effect.

Hume used both historical and philosophical analysis to explain, justify, and praise the rise of the commercial republic. In many ways a rejection of Locke, Hume's theory still used much of Locke's epistemology as well as Hutcheson's theory of moral sentiment in a mix that stood as a primary competitor to the traditional republican emphasis on virtue. Hume's epistemological realism emphasized the analysis of factions and actual human behavior as opposed to republican theory's emphasis on the inculcation of virtues in order to modify human behavior. The republican theorists saw corruption as the primary source of political instability, but Hume believed factions to be the chief threat to popular government and the happiness it produced; it is known that Madison borrowed much of his argument in *Federalist* No. 10 from Hume.[17]

Hume provided a philosophical basis for the economic theories we now associate with thinkers like Adam Smith. He also belonged to a group of men who analyzed the economic basis for material progress in human history, a material progress associated with and undergirding the rise and spread of liberty. Others in this group included William Robertson, Adam Ferguson, Lord Kames, James Dunbar, Joseph Addison, Daniel Defoe, John Millar, William Falconer, and Gilbert Stuart. Adam Smith's *Wealth of Nations*, echoing the Scottish Enlightenment's philosophy of self-interest and the economic analysis based upon such a view of human nature, also contributed to the idea of material, social, and political progress. Smith wrote of the move from "rudeness" to "refinement" and argued that human social development had a "natural history," much as the biological world did. Associated with Smith's attempt to develop a theory of political economy were Charles Davenant, John Law, Josiah Child, William Petty, Dudley North, James Steuart Denham, and Adam Anderson. Although these men were read in late eighteenth-century America, they, along with Adam Smith, had their strongest impact after the turn of the nineteenth century.

On the one hand, both Hume and Smith rejected Locke's notion of contract, the state of nature, and rational calculation as the basis for morals. On the other hand, they started with Locke's epistemology found in his *Essay Concerning Human Understanding* and worked from the theory of history implicit in Locke. Many Americans saw in Locke's *Second Treatise on Government* a linear view of history, an emphasis upon economic development as the driving force in history, and the idea that history reveals predictable interactions between human needs and human institutions, interactions mediated by reason. Adam Smith reflects these aspects of

Locke's theoretical reasoning in his *Wealth of Nations*. Note, however, that Locke's influence through Hume and Smith is not a direct transmission of political ideas and institutions from Locke to the founding generation. Furthermore, not Adam Smith, but Hume, Locke's most severe and successful critic, was the most influential of the Scottish philosophers on the founding generation. Hume's direct criticism of Locke had to have at least as much of a negative effect on Locke's reputation as Hume's borrowing of certain assumptions from Locke's philosophy resulted in a positive effect.

The Enlightenment

Terms like "republicanism" and "liberalism" were developed years later by historians as labels for intellectual movements composed of thinkers who shared a significant number of assumptions, goals, and principles. The term "Enlightenment," however, was coined by the people to whom it presumably referred as a self-description, and it was used by later historians as a label for an entire era. The intent of those thinkers who developed the term was to distinguish their movement from the dark ages of ignorance and superstition that preceded them and thereby to provide an implicit invidious comparison with their political enemies—those people who defended traditional values, methods, and institutions.

One practical consequence of the political agenda implied by the term Enlightenment was to include those individuals who rejected or seemed to reject the old ways of thinking, regardless of their position. As a result, those thinkers associated with the Enlightenment exhibited a melange of approaches, a cacophony of ideas. Names so appropriated included idealists like George Berkeley, rationalists like Descartes, scientists like Newton, realists like Locke, and a wild variety of physiocrats, free traders, utilitarians, classicists, philosophical skeptics, romantics, moralists, atheists, churchmen, empiricists, mathematicians, liberals, democrats, aristocrats, and just about every other discernible group.

Enlightenment thinkers certainly emphasized human reason or rationality, and they often emphasized secular as opposed to religious assumptions. This general characterization sometimes hides more than it reveals, however. The thinkers like Descartes who emphasized reason were not especially innovative in this regard, for men like William of Ockham had been rationalists centuries earlier; instead, the modern rationalists were distinguished by their numbers and by their radical insistence upon rationalist premises. Since an equally important part of the Enlightenment was the rise of science and social science based upon empirical reason as opposed to pure reason, however, the Enlightenment as an intellectual movement was quite diverse in its epistemology. Could one arrive at truth using only analytical logic along the lines of "I think, therefore I am," or was truth limited to that which could be systematically observed through the senses? There was no single Enlightenment answer to the question.

Also, though a strong antireligious bias was evident in the writings of many thinkers during the era, working from secular, rationalist premises is not the same as being antireligious. Many famous writers during the Enlightenment were quite frankly religious both personally and in their work. Locke may have deemphasized religion, but many of his readers find God prominent in his political theory. Isaac Newton, after divining the laws of mechanics, spent the last thirty years of his life studying and writing about the Bible.

In sum, to say that the founders were strongly influenced by the Enlightenment amounts to saying little more than that the variety of European thinkers writing between 1670 and 1787 had an impact on the political theory of the American founding; the triviality of the statement is matched by its potential for confusing the unwary. The strategy here, then, is to subdivide the Enlightenment in a way that allows a meaningful and sensible examination of the influences on American thought beyond those already identified.

One useful method of categorization might distinguish four "enlightenments": a radical, antireligious strain that tended to emphasize pure reason; a natural-religion strain that attacked religious orthodoxy but was more interested in updating religion to be congruent with modern, empirical views of human nature than in rejecting religion; a moderate, liberal or constitutional strain that used both rationalism and empiricism and often emphasized the importance of economics; and a scientific or empirical strain that took advances in natural science as its model for advancing human knowledge about social, political, and economic matters.[18]

As one might expect, even with the mutually contradictory characteristics of these categories, it is often difficult to place a given thinker cleanly in one or the other groups with any great confidence.

The first group, which included men like Voltaire, Diderot, and Helvetius, can be dealt with quickly. Although the works of these men were certainly known to the best-educated Americans, they were not widely read and had little if any influence on the writing of the Constitution.

The second group was in certain respects quite diverse, although their consistent impact was to deemphasize the antagonism between religion and the natural world. This approach allowed religious people to pursue life relatively free from biblical constraints and to be more concerned with practical effects, which were generally seen as either outside the moral realm or compatible with Christian morality. Members of this group were proponents of "rational Christianity," who frequently saw self-interested behavior as compatible with religion and tended to limit religion to devotional practices at certain times of the week. The group included John Tillotson, Samuel Clarke, Joseph Butler, Matthew Tindal, William Paley, Philip Doddridge, John Toland, and William Wollaston. The impact of these writers upon American thinking was cumulative and indirect. Certainly a number of prominent Federalists were Deists, as were a number of writers in this group. Yet their major influence on Federalist and Antifederalist thinking was to reinforce the notion, pressed from other quarters as well, that the proper analysis of politics did not require reference to God's will or to explicitly religious principles.

Members of the third or "moderate" group in the Enlightenment were notable for reflecting explicitly upon political institutions, processes, and assumptions, although often in a piecemeal or specialized fashion. They also shared an interest in or inclination toward constitutional or liberal democracy, as we now call it. Beccaria, Burlamaqui, Delolme, Grotius, Mably, Raynal, and Vattel were prominent in this category; Rousseau might be placed here or among the more radical figures, although his work was not widely read and did not have much influence until after the writing of the Constitution. Americans of the founding era turned to these moderate Enlightenment figures for ideas on specific institutions or problems such as checks and balances, prison reform, slavery, methods of holding elections, taxation, free trade, and for definitions of a republic and of citizenship. Interestingly, aside from a marked interest in Grotius, the Federalists did not cite members of this group as frequently as the Antifederalists did.

The fourth group within the Enlightenment was by far the most influential on the founders' thinking, although it is not always clear who should be placed in it—certainly Montesquieu and Pufendorf, probably Locke as a result of his *Essay Concerning Human Understanding*, and, although he would not like the company, Hume. Each of these thinkers could also be placed in at least one other category of influence on the Federalists. Hume is often placed squarely within the Scottish Enlightenment; indeed, his presence in that group helped lead to its being called the Scottish *Enlightenment*, although it is also called the Scottish Common Sense tradition. Locke is also considered part of the liberal and republican Whig traditions. Pufendorf is frequently considered a liberal, as is Montesquieu, although the latter is often thought to be a civic humanist, or republican, as well. Take your pick. I am here using these categories as a means of identifying the various Enlightenment influences upon the founders, not as a means of definitively locating each figure in the history of ideas. Montesquieu was the author most frequently cited by Federalist as well as Antifederalist; they took from him a number of specific constitutional and institutional ideas. Locke stood as deep background for the Federalists, as did Pufendorf. The borrowing from Hume with respect to specific institutions was narrow but extremely important since it included the notion of the extended republic and the method of analyzing factions. Aside from the borrowing of specific ideas and institutions, however, this fourth group is important for the entire analysis in *The Federalist* insofar as it linked the Federalists with science and induced in them a desire for a science of politics. This influence is so important, so little appreciated, and so frequently missed altogether that it merits expanded treatment here as a separate category.

Science and Politics

The seventeenth century saw the rise of modern, experimental science in the person not only of Newton but also of men like William Harvey and Robert Boyle. Foremost among its proponents was Francis Bacon, who extended rational, empirical techniques to philosophy and the analysis of politics. Newton's discoveries captured the imagination of the age and, combined with Bacon's vision of a social science, led many thinkers to hope they could discover fundamental laws for politics as Newton had done for physics. Among these men were Montesquieu, Hume, and Pufendorf. In a somewhat less directly observational vein, Hobbes, Locke, Rousseau, and Blackstone pursued the discovery of a set of basic human laws of political behavior—whether based on pure reason, the shrewd estimation and summary of observed human behavior, intuition, moral sentiment, or the historical usages of the common law.

Montesquieu, Hume, and Pufendorf spoke explicitly of a "political science" or a "science of politics," as did Publius. Each was inclined to survey the entirety of human history, not for the usual historian's purpose of explaining a given historical phenomenon by discovering the events leading up to it but to uncover in human history regularities of behavior from which could be deduced laws similar to those Newton had deduced from observing the movement of heavenly bodies, Boyle from observing chemical reactions, and Harvey from observing the flow of blood. In each of these three cases, the scientist began with the observation of regularities, deduced laws to explain them, predicted on the basis of the laws further phenomena not yet observed but observable, and then moved to the experimental testing of the predicted phenomena.

The Federalists tended to be counted among those who saw the possibility of a science of politics. Hume and Montesquieu were only two of many writers who contributed to this notion, but they were easily the most influential. Americans learned from these men that humans display regularities in behavior that are compounded of simple, fundamental propensities in their common nature and certain central aspects of their environment and that political institutions are critical aspects of the total environment. Bacon had worked out the formula earlier, and Hobbes, Locke, and Rousseau had each developed a philosophically coherent and rhetorically dramatic theory of political behavior based upon a few simple principles; but Montesquieu and Hume, especially Montesquieu, provided detailed analysis that explicitly

linked human nature, the human environment, and political institutions with a variety of regularities in human behavior.

When reading *The Federalist* and other writings from the
founding era, one cannot help but be struck by the appearance of
three widely held assumptions: (1) There is order in the universe,
(2) we can know that order through the use of observation and
reason, and (3) we can use that natural order in constructing our
political institutions. Even ministers reflected these assumptions
in their sermons and were not loathe to cite Newton and Locke as
well as Saints Peter and Paul. The Divine Law, based upon revelation, and the laws of nature, derived from scientific reasoning,
were seen by most ministers of the time to be different reflections
of God's mind and thus in harmony instead of in conflict.

There is also a strong sense in *The Federalist* and many other
writings of the founding era, both Federalist and Antifederalist, of
each political institution being in the nature of an "experiment"
whose effectiveness will be determined by observation. The concept earlier identified as "experience" amounts to using observation, made systematic by reason, to test an institution, which embodies a hypothesis about human behavior. Many founders
viewed the Constitution as a complex institutional mechanism,
adjustable on the basis of changes in the environment, to over-
come flaws revealed by experience. In this context the amendment
process becomes an important part of the Constitution, and we
are led to understand why such a radically new device in constitutional history did not cause controversy at the Constitutional Convention—it simply reflected a deeply and widely held perception
of politics as an experimental science.

The metaphor of constitution as machine or mechanistic device was widely used but intermixed with a more biological or organic metaphor. A "system" can be clocklike, with gears, wheels,
and levers; but it can also be, just as a human body, a tree, or a solar system, beyond human manipulation. The Federalists saw a
constitution as mixing human invention with natural processes.
Man-made political institutions hemmed in, governed, chan-
neled, directed, or activated natural human inclinations and social
processes, so a political system was simultaneously biological and
mechanistic.

The connection between the natural sciences and the "science of politics," as the phrase was put in *The Federalist*, was a commonplace in political discourse during the entire founding era. For example, a striking exchange took place between John Dickinson and James Wilson at the Constitutional Convention on June 7, 1787. John Dickinson, wrote Madison in his notes, "compared the proposed National System to the Solar System, in which the States were the planets, and ought to be left to move freely in their proper orbits. The Gentleman from Pa. (Mr. Wilson) wished he said to extinguish these planets." James Wilson replied:

He was not, however, for extinguishing these planets as was supposed by Mr. D[ickinson]. Neither did he on the other hand believe that they would warm or enlighten the Sun. Within their proper orbits they must still be suffered to act for subordinate purposes for which their existence is made essential by the great extent of our Country.

Continuing the next day (June 8, 1787), James Madison said:

Experience has evinced a constant tendency in the states to encroach on the federal authority. . . . A negative was the mildest expedient that could be devised for preventing these mischiefs. . . . In a word, to recur to the illustrations borrowed from the planetary System. This prerogative of the General Government is the greatest pervading principle that must control the centrifugal tendencies of the States; which without it, will continually fly out of their proper orbits and destroy the order and harmony of the political system.[19]

The Federalist is typical in being replete with terminology taken from the Newtonian heritage that Montesquieu and Hume helped transmit. Often the terminology is used metaphorically as in the preceding comments, but more frequently words like "tendency," "revolution," "balance," "equilibrium," "fulcrum," "system," "reaction," "mass," "power," and many other terms derived from science are used with the precise meaning and intent of a physical scientist.

 There are important consequences for interpreting Madison's notes on the Constitutional Convention, *The Federalist*, and thus the U.S. Constitution, if we read these terms scientifically. First, the aspects of the document that are puzzling today become more comprehensible. For example, the term "balance," as in checks and balances, meant a mechanism for regulating the speed at which a process or an operation takes place. A balance was not a balance scale but a balance beam, as in a watch, that allowed the main sprocket wheel to advance one cog at a time. A balance, therefore, allowed a process to go forward but not at an unregulated rate. The precise use of scientific terminology was also associated with important conceptual advances. For example, political power had usually been seen as belonging to the sovereign, and thus, like sovereignty, not divisible. In physics, however, power is an attribute that can increase or decrease and move from one object to another; it can also be distributed among several entities. Such a view of power as a force that can be split and shifted instead of as an attribute of one entity at a time allowed the Federalists and Antifederalists to see how power could be separated into discrete amounts among several entities or distributed among several branches and levels of government.

The mechanistic, scientific strand in the thinking of the founders can be traced to many writers, including Hobbes, Locke, Hume, and Montesquieu as well as to Bacon, Newton, Priestley, Harvey, and Boyle. If any aspect of the founders' intellectual heritage has been ignored more than Calvinist Christianity, it is the contribution of a developing science to American political theory.

Relative Influence

Although there is no sure and easy way to summarize the relative impact of these various influences on the founders, a count of the citations in the political literature produced during the founding era provides a useful overview. The general sample used here covers the period from 1760 to 1805 and includes more than 916 pamphlets, books, and newspaper essays with 3,154 references to 224 different individuals. The sample includes virtually all the pamphlets and essays from the 1780s by Federalists and Antifederalists concerning the Constitution.[20]

Even though the definition of intellectual traditions is not en-

Table 5.1.   Distribution of Citations by Decade (in percent)

Category	1760s	1770s	1780s	1790s	1800–1805	Total N
Bible	24	44	34	29	38	34
Enlightenment	32 (21)	18 (11)	24 (23)	21 (20)	18 (17)	22 (19)
Whig	10 (21)	20 (27)	19 (20)	17 (18)	15 (16)	18 (21)
Common Law	12	4	9	14	20	11
Classical	8	11	10	11	2	9
Other	14	3	4	8	7	6
	100	100	100	100	100	100
	$n=216$	$n=544$	$n=1306$	$n=674$	$n=414$	$N=3154$

Note: The categorization scheme used here is basically that developed by Bernard Bailyn.
Source: Donald S. Lutz, "The Relative Influence of European Writers on Late Eighteenth Century American Political Thought," American Political Science Review 78 (March 1984):189–97.

tirely efficacious and granting that the assignment of authors and citations to a given category will vary somewhat, depending upon who is doing the assigning, one can conclude that no apparent basis exists for identifying any category of thinkers as dominant or decisive in its influence on the founders (see Table 5.1). Also, the members of a given category might be construed as contributing to one or more other categories. For example, Blackstone supplemented and extended classical liberalism, and at the same time he saw himself engaged in a quasi-scientific enterprise, much as those thinkers in the fourth subcategory of the European Enlightenment. Hume belongs squarely in the Scottish Enlightenment, but he too was pursuing ends similar to those in this fourth, "politics as a science," group of the European Enlightenment.

If we break Bernard Bailyn's Enlightenment category into the three subcategories described by Lundberg and May, the results are not significantly altered. The First Enlightenment, dominated by Montesquieu, Locke, and Pufendorf, comprises 16 percent of all citations. The more radical writers of the Second Enlightenment, men like Voltaire, Diderot, and Helvetius, garner 2 percent of the citations. The Third Enlightenment, typified by Beccaria, Rousseau, Mably, and Raynal, includes 4 percent of the citations, to bring the total back to the 22 percent listed on Table 5.1 for all Enlightenment writers. Bailyn's scheme is one of the most prominent but still subject to controversy. For example, where should Locke

Table 5.2.   Order of Rank by Frequency of Citation (in percent)

1.	Montesquieu	8.3	19.	Shakespeare	0.8
2.	Blackstone	7.9	20.	Livy	0.8
3.	Locke	2.9	21.	Pope	0.7
4.	Hume	2.7	22.	Milton	0.7
5.	Plutarch	1.5	23.	Tacitus	0.6
6.	Beccaria	1.5	24.	Coxe	0.6
7.	Trenchard and		25.	Plato	0.5
	Gordon (Cato)	1.4	26.	Raynal	0.5
8.	Delolme	1.4	27.	Mably	0.5
9.	Pufendorf	1.3	28.	Machiavelli	0.5
10.	Coke	1.3	29.	Vattel	0.5
11.	Cicero	1.2	30.	Petyt	0.5
12.	Hobbes	1.0	31.	Voltaire	0.5
13.	Robertson	0.9	32.	Robinson	0.5
14.	Grotius	0.9	33.	Sidney	0.5
15.	Rousseau	0.9	34.	Somers	0.5
16.	Bolingbroke	0.9	35.	Harrington	0.5
17.	Bacon	0.8	36.	Rapin-Thoyras	0.5
18.	Price	0.8			

Source: Lutz, "Relative Influence of European Writers," 189–97.

be placed? Shifting Locke to the category of Whigs, as many or most of the founders perceived him, changes the percentages to those in parentheses on the table.

One major conclusion we can draw from this table is that the impact of religion and biblical sources on American political theory needs to be examined carefully. Notwithstanding the importance of separating church from state in our politics, it would appear that students of American political theory ignore the impact of religion only at the cost of missing an important influence. The sample here is designed to illustrate the relative impact of European secular thinkers, and therefore it largely excludes political pamphlets and tracts that were reprinted sermons, even though at least 80 percent of the political pamphlets during the 1770s and 1780s were written by ministers.[21] Even excluding the majority of sermons that had no references to secular thinkers, as we have done here, Deuteronomy is the most frequently cited book, followed by Montesquieu's *The Spirit of the Laws*.

The works of the thirty-six men listed in Table 5.2 drew one half of the citations, and those of twenty-two more writers virtually tie for thirty-seventh place and together account for another 10 percent of the citations. The list of secular authors has more than 180 additional names; those just below the cutoff for Table 5.2 are Burlamaqui, Godwin, Adam Smith, Volney, Shaftesbury, Hooker, Burlingame, Hoadley, Molesworth, Priestley, Macaulay, Goldsmith, Hutcheson, Burgh, Defoe, Paley, Ferguson, Fortescue, Virgil, Polybius, Aristotle, and Thucydides. There is a certain asymmetry since the first four names in Table 5.2 account for one-third of all the citations attributable to the top fifty-eight names, which implies that the contributions of these four need to be considered more carefully. Otherwise, the apparent parity among a large number of names from supposedly different intellectual "traditions" and the almost random mixing of the names reflect the way we find them in the literature. One does not find references grouped in a given pamphlet according to republican, liberal, or Enlightenment categories but scattered over many names in a seeming haphazard fashion.

An unusual aspect of the list, one that deserves emphasis, is that Locke's prominence is due largely to reprinted sermons by ministers. The forty-one sermons that cited at least one secular author amounted to a little less than 5 percent of the items in the total sample and about 9 percent of the 446 pamphlets in the sample. These sermons together accounted for almost 20 percent of the citations to secular authors, including just about half of the references to John Locke. If we exclude the references to Locke generated by ministers, his count falls to about 1.5 percent of the total, which places him between Beccaria and Trenchard and Gordon, whose positions in the ranking are not affected by dropping the sermons. The rank of no other name in Table 5.2 is affected by more than one or two places in the order by excluding the reprinted sermons. One interesting implication is that those defending the importance of Locke will probably also have to defend the importance of biblically based theology for American political theory during the founding era.

The relative importance of a thinker or a group of thinkers varied according to the time of the founding era in question (see Table 5.3). For example, John Locke was profound on the basis for civil society and the grounds for breaking with a government but had relatively little to say about specific institutions; thus it is not surprising that his influence was most direct on those founders writ-

Table 5.3. Most Cited Secular Thinkers by Decade (in percent)

	1760s	1770s	1780s	1790s	1800–1805	Total N
Montesquieu	8	7	14	4	1	8.3
Blackstone	1	3	7	11	15	7.9
Locke	11	7	1	1	1	2.9
Hume	1	1	1	6	5	2.7
Plutarch	1	3	1	2	0	1.5
Beccaria	0	1	3	0	0	1.5
Cato	1	1	3	0	0	1.4
Delolme	0	0	3	1	0	1.4
Pufendorf	4	0	1	0	5	1.3
Coke	5	0	1	2	4	1.3
Cicero	1	1	1	2	1	1.2
Hobbes	0	1	1	0	0	1.0
Subtotal	33	25	37	29	32	32.4
Others	67	75	63	71	68	67.6
Total	100	100	100	100	100	100.0
	n=216	n=544	n=1306	n=674	n=414	N=3154

Note: The extra decimal point in the last column allows more precise recovery of the number of citations over the era; all other percentages are rounded off to the nearest whole number to ease the viewing of the table. The use of 0 percent indicates less than .5 percent of the citations for a given decade.
Source: Lutz, "Relative Influence of European Writers," 189–97.

ing the Declaration of Independence and only indirect on those writing the Constitution. The Whig historians and theorists were most directly influential during the time that the early state constitutions were being adopted. The Whigs were joined in importance and to a certain degree supplanted by Blackstone, Hume, and Montesquieu by the time the federal Constitution was being drafted and debated. The earlier influences were still present; but because each of these three theorists had much to say about specific institutional designs and each had a deep and coherent analysis of republican government in general and the British political system in particular, they had a special, independent impact upon the thinking of those who framed the Constitution.[22]

One basic point to stress is the similarity the Federalists and Antifederalists shared in their intellectual heritage. Not only do we *not* find the Federalists inclined toward Enlightenment writers and the Antifederalists away from them, the Federalists sometimes cited Enlightenment writers only to disagree with them. For example, many Federalists argued against Montesquieu's dictum that re-

Table 5.4. Federalist and Antifederalist Citations (in percent)

	Federalist	Antifederalist	Total for 1780s
Montesquieu	29	25	14
Blackstone	7	9	7
Locke	0	3	1
Hume	3	1	1
Plutarch	7	0	1
Beccaria	0	4	3
Cato	2	2	3
Delolme	0	6	3
Pufendorf	0	1	1
Coke	0	1	1
Cicero	0	1	1
Robertson	0	0	1
Lycurgus	6	1	1
Mably	7	2	2
Grotius	5	0	1
Temple	5	1	1
Price	0	2	1
Addison	0	2	.5
Vattel	0	1	.5
Sidney	1	0	.5
Subtotal	72	62	44.5
Other	28	38	55.5
Total:	100	100	100
	$n = 164$	$n = 364$	$n = 1306$

Source: Lutz, "Relative Influence of European Writers," 189–97.

publics must be small and homogeneous if they are to survive, but the Antifederalists cited Montesquieu with approval. One could argue that the Antifederalists agreed with Montesquieu on this point because it expressed the wisdom of the ancients, which they were more likely to agree with, given their "republicanism," than the more "modern" Federalists; but in fact Federalist literature was more likely than Antifederalist writing to cite the ancients. This tendency and a stronger inclination by the Federalists to use scientific metaphors and to seek a science of politics were the most noticeable differences between Federalist and Antifederalist use of their common intellectual heritage. Still, the differences were more in the nature of tendencies than in distinguishing characteristics.

The similarity in the intellectual heritage used by Federalists and Antifederalists implies two important possibilities. One is that there was a core to American political theory during the founding era that represented a commonly accepted synthesis of the various strands of thought and of the thinkers available to the founders. This synthesis would go far in explaining, for example, why the Antifederalists so quickly turned to supporting a Constitution that they had so bitterly opposed at first. A second possibility is that instead of deep theoretical differences, the division between Federalists and Antifederalists was based upon more ordinary political considerations. One might construe the struggle, for example, as competition between a national, cosmopolitan elite and a set of state-based, localist elites. This interpretation would make the ideas and arguments advanced by the many European thinkers and traditions a coin of the realm to be used in a political debate where the currency was indeed common and therefore possibly spendable, or persuasive.

The founders ransacked these various intellectual traditions for ideas that they appropriated and blended in the service of solving American problems in a manner congruent with their own constitutional tradition arising from their own experience. In short, they tended to use history and the history of ideas just as we do today—sometimes in the service of political or ideological goals but often in the service of a search for enduring truth about how to create and maintain a government that has the power needed to be effective as well as the justice needed to preserve popular consent.

Chapter 6

Prolegomenon

Plato long ago suggested that the first step in the journey to knowledge consists in distinguishing appearance from reality, illusion from truth. A fork, when placed in a glass of water, may appear to bend, but a theoretical physics based on the assumption that "solid objects bend when placed in water" does not go very far. By the same token, before one can engage in American political theory it is necessary that certain facts be rehearsed and working assumptions examined, so that even if we do not agree on where to begin we do not unconsciously or uncritically begin with equivalents to the water-bends-solids premise, such as the assumption that political theories are only ideologies or that texts in political theory must always be approached as complete and ideal. A pretheoretical analysis that undergirds, informs, and directs inquiry is a necessary part of true theoretical thinking; the previous chapters are designed to contribute to a pretheoretical analysis of American political theory.

The analysis reveals a number of assumptions that must be examined. How we answer the questions that result from a confrontation with these assumptions will determine how we define the discipline, and so it is worth our assembling here an overview of the position that is being offered. To sharpen the discussion, the position will be presented as a series of premises that read like theorems or settled propositions, although it should be remembered that the premises are not designed as assumptions to be accepted as much as they are matters that need to be addressed more explicitly.

First Premise: Any theory worthy of the name is a claim for some truth that transcends not only its historical era but also its culture and the intent of its creator. I have focused this discussion heavily on the American founding era because it is the preface to 200 years of American political events and theoretical analysis. Also, space does not permit a discussion of American political theory since 1800. Yet the implications of the first premise include the absolute necessity that the study of American political theory cover the entire American experience, from 1620 to the present, not just the founding era, for two reasons. First, a theory that is true can be supported by evidence from any era and in fact must be so if its truth is to be established. It will not do to claim that a certain generation or a certain group had a special hold on the truth and we must believe what they say because *they* said it. Second, the political thinking of the founding era was grounded in theory that came before it and that has been confirmed or modified by thinking that came after it. We do ourselves no favors by pretending that the nineteenth century was a wasteland in American political thinking or that the twentieth century is only the source of theoretical perversity. A complete preface to American political theory would include a beginning list of post-1800 texts worth our attention, a task that has yet to be carried out adequately by anyone.

Just as we should not seek the intentions of the founders under the assumption that a special genius automatically makes their theories true, neither should we reject the truth of their theories based on any personal failings they may have had. It is a logical fallacy to accept or reject an act or an idea because of its source—the genetic fallacy. Yet there are those who, with a straight face, indulge in the following logical sequence:

Major premise: A person who does a bad thing cannot produce anything that is of value or is true.

Minor premise: Person "A" has done a bad thing.

Conclusion: Person "A" cannot have produced anything of value or said anything that is true.

If a man proves to be a "womanizer" or a woman a "manizer," we, as American political theorists, should be able to distinguish our dismay and approbation over that person's casual and predatory treatment of members of the opposite sex or flaunting of marriage vows or both from our estimation of the truth and utility of that person's political theory. Truth, like beauty, does not depend upon the intentions or character of the person who offers it; otherwise, we would examine the moral life of Mozart, Einstein, Meryl Streep, or Billie Jean King before judging whether to appreciate their music, science, acting, or tennis. The same principle, it would seem, applies to the political theories of John C. Calhoun, Abraham Lincoln, Herbert Croly, and Martin Luther King.

Similarly, we should treat slaveholding with the opprobrium it deserves but distinguish our anger and disappointment in this regard from the truth that may be found in the theoretical political thinking of those people who owned slaves, or who did not own slaves but failed to condemn it, or who condemned it but failed to act effectively against it. There are gradations of evil, and slavery has to rank high on the scale, but logic that is true and useful to humans with lesser failings should not be rejected solely on the grounds that the theory is generated by someone whose sins are greater. If the evil in a person's life informs and warps his or her theory, as has been concluded about Adolph Hitler, we can then reject the theory on its own merits. Our experience has shown that the political theory underlying the U.S. Constitution was not warped but has led Americans to inevitable, straightforward conclusions that required the elimination of slavery, the expansion of the electorate, and the broadening of rights. One does not have to read very far in the pamphlet literature of the 1780s to discover that many members of the active political class, north and south, were perfectly well aware of these deductions. Still, as is often the case, the theory was strong, but the political will was weak.

Second Premise: American political theory can be defined as the normative, analytic, and empirical study of American political texts, institutions, processes, issues, and values derived from and defined by its constitutional tradition. This working definition of the discipline contains a number of crucial points. One aspect, the blending of empirical, normative, and analytic concerns, deserves extended comment. Political theory properly understood is not opposed to the empirical study of politics but encompasses it. Indeed, American political theory, because it rests upon the analysis of experience, requires the development of data-based analysis using sophisticated mathematical and statistical techniques. At the same time, because American political theory engages in the constant evaluation of the American experiment and aims at improving the capacity of the experiment to achieve its ends, the discipline requires that empirical study be driven by theory that explains why a given empirical question is worth studying and that evaluates the results in a context that has normative implications. Empiricists, despite disclaimers, always end up, often covertly, putting their findings in such a context; and normative theorists inevitably make use of factual statements if their words are to have any relationship to the world in which we live but frequently use empirical statements in an unsystematic or unexamined fashion. The tendency by both sides to view their questions and approach as the only legitimate one rests ultimately upon a peculiar logic about life.

Imagine a person who spends her day earning a living as an accountant. Imagine that person coming home and using the same methodology on the family as at work—calculating the costs and benefits of spouse and children to see if their "costs and benefits to the life of the accountant" balance. Imagine now that same accountant going to work and using "family logic" to sort numbers on the basis of how she feels about them, preferring, for example, the number six, to which she has developed an attachment or fondness, over the number three, which once let the accountant down by being misplaced. Or imagine a physician using techniques of close textual analysis on his patients or in dealings with the spouse and kids.

Life does not allow us to use the same approach in every circumstance any more than it presents us with morally perfect people whose political theories we can then adopt in preference to those devised by evil people. Life is messy, often lacks logic, and presents us with a multitude of problems and opportunities that yield to approaches appropriate to each. Why should we expect that American political theory will be an exception to life and be any more susceptible to a single, universally applicable approach? In order to defend such an exceptional view political scientists of one persuasion or another inevitably are pushed to the position that certain questions are "trivial" or "not worth asking"; or, in its milder form, certain questions are "not very interesting." The deep structure of such a response, ultimately, is to say that life is not interesting, since life presents us with questions, problems, and challenges that will not yield to a single "nontrivial" or "interesting" perspective.

There are many scholars in political science who see the divisions as being far more than methodological in origin. Some insist that the normative approach is inherently oppressive since it seeks to explain or enforce values that can be only personal and idiosyncratic; others insist that empirical research somehow fiddles with nature and corrupts our moral vision. The arguments here are unlikely to change many of these minds, nor is that the intent. Rather, the intent is to suggest that the discipline of American political theory requires us to remain open to a variety of systematic approaches that together reflect our total experience of life. It is the discipline of architects who cannot ignore the laws of physics that underlie lines of loadbearing any more than they can ignore the factual characteristics of each material used in construction or the aesthetics of design. It is a discipline of integration and synthesis.

A complete preface to American political theory would show how to link empirical research with analytic and normative concerns. Historical research is one form of empirical inquiry, but what I have in mind here includes behavioral and aggregate data analysis using the most advanced statistical and methodological techniques. In the absence of space to develop a full model one could point to the work of Calvin Jillson as one of many examples. Jillson applied factor-analytic techniques typically used in legislative roll-call analysis to examine roll-call coalitions in the 1787 Constitutional Convention in Philadelphia.[1] His systematic empirical approach allows him to identify voting coalitions, to determine that there were several realignments during the Convention—each resulting in a new coalition over a number of issues—and to sort out the mix of principles and interests that went into the final accommodation. Along the way he puts to rest several puzzles or debates that historians had developed in working with different techniques. Jillson's book, when read together with other studies that work from close textual analysis of primary theoretical tracts, illustrates how empirical research can be generated and guided by questions raised through other methodologies and then made to serve and support textual and historical analyses with quite explicit normative implications.

Another example of such integrated research might be Christian Bay's *The Structure of Freedom,* in which the author analyzes the components of a definition of freedom, conducts a comprehensive exploration of the empirical literature of the social sciences for evidence relevant to the implications of his analysis, and discusses the normative implications of his findings.[2]

Of course, empirical research is not limited to the use of data susceptible to statistical analysis. Historical research is an empirical enterprise that attempts a systematic analysis of data that frequently are not reducible to numerical form. The same is true of legal research, an important component of and contributor to the enterprise being defined here. American political theory has always worked implicitly from an operational definition of politics based on constitutionalism. Thus, because of the role of the Supreme Court in the American constitutional system, the Court has been a major generator of American political theory since 1800. Therefore, one major implication of the definition that constitutes our second premise is that American political theory must devote a significant amount of its attention to Supreme Court decisions and to their implications.

These decisions establish a data base that can be used to test important empirical propositions in American political theory. Together these decisions also serve as a summary of the changes that American political theory has undergone and of the theoretical positions currently contending for supremacy. An interesting book by Martin Edelman uses Supreme Court decisions as a data base for systematic textual analysis and delineates the competing democratic theories that justices have developed through their legal reasoning in a constitutional context. Edelman's book provides a good example of how analytic, normative, and empirical concerns overlap in American political theory, how they need to be addressed using a variety of appropriate methods, and how a constitutional context provides a useful focus for distinguishing theoretical positions that would otherwise be abstract and amorphous.[3]

The nature of constitutionalism and its importance for American political theory require that our enterprise blend normative, analytic, and empirical research, which leads us to the next premise.

Third Premise: To define American political theory in terms of consti-

tutionalism means that the empirical study of human behavior in light of popularly approved ends and process stands at the center of the enterprise. Although this premise has already been discussed, it is worth considering the assumptions that underlie it. The idea of constitutionalism, properly understood, assumes (1) that humans can together design a binding, mutually acceptable political process based upon reflection and choice, (2) that constitutions define the political process and the general ends that have been so chosen and accepted, (3) that constitutions and the laws derived from them generate collective human behavior with predictable patterns, and (4) that this behavior ought to be congruent with the ends and process consented to by those humans whose behavior is being structured.

Among those scholars who study constitutions a tendency exists to treat them either as a set of philosophical principles that establishes prescriptive goals or as a set of legalistic doctrines that can be used as trump cards in resolving political controversy. The first tendency belongs to those whose training is in the more traditional political philosophy; the second is typical of those who teach in law schools. Neither tendency is perverse, but together they still add up to an inadequate understanding of constitutions.

Constitutions summarize the relationship that experience and reflection have thus far shown to exist between institutional design and the resulting patterns of political behavior. For example, bicameralism does not rest upon a free-floating philosophical principle but upon a set of ideas connected theoretically, which experience has shown results in a certain pattern of legislative behavior. To the extent that the institutional design is viewed as causing a pattern of behavior, to that extent it also provides an explanation for it. In this sense the set of constitutional rules that define an institution stand as a prediction, as an empirically testable hypothesis, that a certain pattern of behavior will result. Institutions that remain stable over time imply that the resulting behavioral pattern is more or less in line with expectations, and they also imply continuing approval for the predicted pattern of behavior—that we choose this pattern as preferable to any other known alternative.

Therefore, in order to understand the normative prescriptions in a constitution, we need to do more than focus on the more obviously normative statements such as those in a bill of rights. Until and unless we understand the predicted patterns of behavior contained in the institutions defined by the constitution and the manner in which these patterns interact, we will not understand which behavior is preferred and thus which precept is normatively sought.

By the same token, to treat constitutional provisions merely as trump cards is to focus upon winning an argument rather than upon understanding the extent to which political behavior is congruent with predictions or preferences or both. The trump-card approach also is inclined to view the trumping passage in isolation from the rest of the constitution and thus to read it out of context. Constitutions are made up of interlocking institutions and therefore of interacting patterns of behavior; any piece of the pattern must be understood as part of a whole.

Finally, the constitutional approach puts empirical political scientists on notice that their methodology is critically important because the predicted behavioral patterns mediate between the normative, philosophical theorizing and the use of constitutions as the trump card. Without the behavioral understanding to connect them, the normative and legal aspects float free. At the same time, the constitutional approach imposes upon empiricists the responsibility to investigate the important as opposed to the trivial and to conduct research in such a way that operational definitions are compatible enough to result in cumulative knowledge. Until or unless empirical political science becomes part of a larger project that brings it greater coherence, it too will tend to float free. The centrality of constitutionalism to American political theory results also in the next premise.

Fourth Premise: The constitutions, documents, and writings upon which American political theory is built require that we construct complete texts that cannot be studied the same way as philosophical texts. How we assemble a text and the use we make of the text we assemble are crucially affected by the attitude we bring to it. The implications of this premise have been discussed in chapter 3, but one implication in particular deserves a little more explication. The analysis shows that the authors of constitutions and other writing designed for public understanding and approval must consider the meaning that would be supplied by an active citizenry. That is, the meaning of a political text in a system based upon popular control is a function of the interplay between the author's intended meaning, the words as written, and the citizens' appropriation. Analysis of texts in American political theory thus cannot meaningfully proceed from the stance of an indifferent philosopher but must proceed instead from the stance of an interested, educated citizen. Since a citizen's education results prominently from participation in politics, the manner and extent of citizen participation takes on particular importance in American political theory. Finally, then, American political theory inherently involves analysis of democratic and republican theory.

In other words, American political theory inevitably involves itself with questions concerning a string of concepts that, when properly understood, lead inexorably to each other. One can conceive of such a string of concepts beginning with the concept most fundamental to democratic theory, popular sovereignty, followed by political participation, political equality, majority rule, individual and minority rights, the common good, political virtue, representation, deliberative processes, procedural fairness, effective institutional design, liberty, and a government that combines justice with power. Although the list is not meant to be exhaustive, it does set forth basic concepts that lie at the core of our concern.

That these concepts are central to American political theory explains and justifies our continuing interest in the study of such matters as electoral behavior, legislative process and behavior, public-policy evaluation, interest-group behavior, the operation of political parties, the status and treatment of minorities, public law and judicial behavior, and so on. To put it most clearly, our concept of modern political science is the direct result of American political theory defining what subjects are worth our study as well as strongly inclining us to use systematic empirical methods. European political science differs in its methods and objects of study precisely to the extent that it is not guided by American political theory; the extent to which overlap exists between American political science and political science elsewhere results from others adopting the research agenda that has been defined by American political theory.

Opposition to the integrated, constitutional approach that is distinctively American rests ultimately upon European perspectives that are in some sense hostile to American political theory. One such European perspective, which is based upon the extreme logical positivism developed by the Vienna Circle, supports American empiricism but neglects or rejects the assumptions that underlie American commitments to liberty, the organization of a free people for collective political ends, and the evaluation of those ends by standards that are not merely ideological, irrational, or grounded in psychological self-interest. The other European perspective, which has its roots in the European idealist tradition, supports the American commitment to a higher law and the insistence upon a value context for political activity, but it is hostile to American insistence that political theory be grounded in experience and built upon the consent of the many as opposed to the imposition from above of an agenda developed by a few great minds who are more able to understand the requirements of reason. The former European-derived position defines the extreme empiricist wing; the latter defines the extreme philosophical wing in the study of American politics. The former tends to deny the relevance for politics of any human experience that is not clearly reducible to a statement of fact, and the latter tends to deny the relevance of experience that is not conformable to a coherent theory developed by a great European mind. Each position, for its own reasons, sees the study of history as worthless at best, if not pernicious. Each brings its own attitude to the analysis of a political text, the first to reject the text as worthy of study, the second to enshrine the text. Not to be confused with these positions are the extreme left and right ideological perspectives in American political theory derived from European Marxist or Nietzschean sources.

On the other hand, American political theory, as we have seen in the earlier discussion on the origin of the Bill of Rights and in the analysis on American use of European political writing, suggests a different operating premise.

Fifth Premise: American constitutionalism, and thus American political theory, although resting in part on English and other European sources, is grounded most importantly in American experience, American needs, and thus in American history, which makes the study of history an essential part of American political theory. The peculiar relevance of American history for American political theory results from the very nature of our political culture. Our theoretical thinking rests upon our own experience, our collective experience of living together as a people, and our experience in self-government. Too many students who begin their academic lives in philosophy fail to appreciate how central this last point is. Because Americans have been a self-governing people, their history is the story of their own attempts at collective self-definition, and thus their story cannot be appropriated to the theory of some philosopher who has not had their experience; instead, philosophical theories must be appropriated by them to their experience. Americans, after reflecting upon their experience, write public documents that embody their collective, agreed-upon sense of selves; the reflection is deepened by other writing surrounding and explaining these documents. The history of these documents and their ancillary writings thus becomes the very stuff of American political theory.

If the job of history is to help us recover the meaning of these writings for those who wrote and read them, the job of American political theory is to help us decide what the meaning in those documents signifies for us today. Obviously, the former must precede the latter; thus American political theorists in political science departments often seem to be historians. Historians explicitly do not wish to work on the latter task, however, and it is at this point that we become political theorists.

The continued appropriation of a meaning by citizens over generations makes an idea or a theory timeless. Political theorists look for regularities and enduring patterns; historians seek an explanation for events that are viewed as discrete, independent, and unrepeatable. In looking for these stable patterns, political theorists make use of history in a way that historians cannot and will not. History is for American political theory the repository of data. In this sense, behavioral research by political scientists is a form of history since it establishes facts that can be reflected upon as well as examined for enduring patterns, and thus all empirically oriented political scientists are contemporary historians.

Still, the key point is that although those scholars working in American political theory can study and in some small way contribute to the enterprise, since American political theory is grounded in the experience of a people who are self-governing, in the end American political theory is defined by the people. Americans tell their own story, define their own values, create their own institutions, and establish their own political theory in the documents that they together approve. There is no evidence that Americans decide which European political philosopher to adopt whole-sale as their own; instead, members of the political class work up competing theoretical syntheses that are presented for approval. A theoretical position is not accepted on the basis of philosophical niceties but because it meets the needs of most of the people, for which we can read "interests," and is part of a self-conception, part of a story about themselves, that they approve.

Sixth Premise: American political theory is grounded in, conditioned by, and ultimately approved by a self-governing, self-defining people. This prem-ise raises questions about the function of those individuals who work in a discipline of American political theory if the enterprise belongs to the people. Essentially we play a multifaceted yet specialized role within the active political class. Through our writing we assist histo-rians in the recovery of original meaning, offer interpretations of the American experience, suggest extensions or alterations in the theory that take into account changing circumstances, and pass this on to oth-ers in the politically active class. We teach our students how to read texts for original meaning, how to systematically reflect upon the American experience, how to interpret this experience (as well as intro-duce them to the major interpretations currently in contention), and perhaps most important we teach our students how to become mem-bers of the politically active class, which brings us to our final premise.

Seventh Premise: The study of American political theory would be best served by focusing more broadly on the writing and activities of the active political class. Premise seven is required by the sixth premise. If a people are self-governing and their self-government is em-bodied in an evolving set of public documents that rests upon their consent, then it would seem perverse to focus American po-litical theory upon a study of writings by a tiny elite. A portion of the population plays a disproportionate role in the design, opera-tion, and analysis of the American political system. Far too nu-merous to be called an elite, the political activist class interprets and organizes politics for the rest of the population and interprets and organizes the needs and demands of the broader population for presentation to those in government. These people together carry in their heads American political culture. From the ranks of this active political class come the people who engage in the pro-cess of self-reflection that we call American political theory.

The juxtaposition of the two preceding sentences highlights a final aspect of American political theory that must be addressed in this preface—the relationship of political theory to political myth and the difficulties that result when both are the product of the same part of the population. First we must speak a bit about political culture.

There are basically three ways in which humans learn: directly, indirectly, and symbolically. If I strike a match and put my finger into the flame, the experience of heat and pain is a direct one that leads me to avoid putting my finger in a flame again. If I watch someone else put a finger in the flame and observe the response, I learn indirectly that I should not put my finger in a flame. If, however, I avoid putting my finger in a flame because my parents or others have used language to tell about the pain, I have learned symbolically.

Language is a shared system of symbols that must be taught to the next generation if continued symbolic learning is to take place. Indeed, since culture may be defined as the shared symbol system that is passed from generation to generation, language is the primary cultural artifact. Culture produces a collective orientation or set of attitudes toward various aspects of human experience and the world around us, and therefore political culture refers to the shared orientation or set of attitudes of a people toward the basic elements in their political system that is passed symbolically across generations.

Culture makes society possible, and political culture makes the political system possible. Note that since political culture as a subpart of general culture rests upon the language used to transmit it, the meaning of words and concepts can have a profound effect on how a political system is perceived, evaluated, and operated. At a deeper level, although it is possible to develop a political institution or practice before a word or concept exists to describe it, that institution or practice will require a name if it is to be passed successfully to future generations. Therefore, the creation of new words and concepts and the control of their usage can have a profound effect on politics. In fact, much of politics involves a struggle over the meanings of words and the evaluation of their referents. That is, much if not most of politics is a symbolic struggle or negotiation among people who share a political culture.[4]

The struggle, in its most fundamental form, proceeds at either a mythic or a theoretical level. We need briefly to discuss myth in order to distinguish it from, and then to relate it to, theory. Contrary to the loose usage common in ordinary language, "myth" does not refer to a story or belief that is false or perhaps made up. As one student of myth puts it:

> A myth, I suggest, is an interpretation of what the myth-maker rightly or wrongly takes to be hard fact. It is a device men adopt in order to come to grips with reality; and we can tell that a given account is a myth, not by the amount of truth it contains, but by the fact that it is *believed* to be true and, above all, by the dramatic form into which it is cast.[5]

A myth, then, refers to a shared story or narrative that provides a common understanding of a civil society's origin, its long-term goals, the justification of its institutions, and some sense of a connection with transcendent value or values shared by a people. The mythic form was more formally codified in earlier times, but modern nations have their myths as well. Myths are generated for the simple reason that a political culture must be passed to the next generation, and the mythic form is a highly efficient and effective way of doing this. Although a myth is usually based on facts or actual events, the significance that people give to the facts and events, the meaning they derive and then believe, is the key to myth. The commonly understood meaning, which is the core of the myth, is inevitably an important component of the political culture that is passed on.

Furthermore, as Eric Voegelin suggests, political analysis should begin with the study of a people's attempt at self-definition or self-interpretation.[6] At some point, if a political system is to endure, a people must constitute themselves *as a people* by achieving a shared psychological state in which they recognize themselves as engaged in a common enterprise and as bound together by widely shared commitments, values, interests, and goals. Essentially a people share symbols and myths that provide meaning for their existence and link them to some transcendent order. Far from being the repository of irrationality, these shared symbols and myths are the basis upon which collective, rational action is possible.

Voegelin says that these shared myths and symbols can be found in embryonic form in a people's earliest political expressions and in "differentiated" form in later writings. By studying the political documents of a people, we can watch the gradual unfolding, elaboration, and alteration of the myths and symbols that define them. For example, the "American Dream," the idea that people migrated to American shores in order to improve their condition, to pursue and achieve happiness, is part of our political myth that can be found expressed embryonically in colonial documents, and then in differentiated form in our Declaration of Independence.

The narrative quality of myth, and the place it has in politics, is nicely summarized by David Carr.

> A community exists wherever a narrative account exists of a "we" which has continuous existence through its experiences and activities. When we say that such an account "exists," we mean to say that it gets articulated or formulated, perhaps by only one or a few of the group's members . . . and is accepted or subscribed to by the other members. It is their acceptance that makes them members. Where such a community exists it is constantly in the process . . . of composing and recomposing its own autobiography. Like the autobiography of an individual, such a story seeks a unifying structure for a sequence of experiences and actions. . . . A community at any moment has a sense of its origins and the prospect of its own death as it seeks to articulate its own coherence and integrity over time. Such articulation involves an interplay of formulation and acceptance on the part of the participants. It may also take the form of a kind of negotiation among participants or even between parties to different versions of the group's story.[7]

"Negotiation" may not be the best word. Since attempts to formulate a new myth, alter an old one, or force acceptance of the current myth may threaten the existence of individuals, minorities, or the entire community, these political "negotiations" are often highly charged or conflictful. Much of politics is quite symbolic and proceeds at the mythic level. Examples abound. Characterizing the founders as "Founding Fathers" is part of a mythic narrative that can be threatened by those people who oppose the capitalization as needless deification or who oppose "fathers" as too gender specific. The television series "Roots," like the book, can be seen as an attempt to make Americans of African heritage more explicitly a part of the American story—an alteration in the myth. The addition of Labor Day, Martin Luther King Day, Veterans' Day, and St. Patrick's Day to our national celebrations, official or otherwise, reflects alterations in our national autobiography. What material to put in American history textbooks is not simply an academic matter, since these texts are a means for passing on our mythic autobiography to the next generation.

Political myth is both related to and clearly distinguishable from political theory. Both seek to explain who we are as a people, what we hold in common, what we should and should not do politically, and so on. Political theory, however, tends inherently to undermine the existing political myths. First, political theory works from a careful, systematic study of history, and the factual nature of events is carefully uncovered and insisted upon. Almost no political myth, no matter how factually grounded, will meet the rigorous tests imposed by historians simply because the *meaning* of an event has priority in myth over factual content. Furthermore, political theory, built upon history, attempts to extract meaning that is rational, logical, and removed from the logic of myth.

To a certain extent the same disjunction obtains between all political activity and political science. Those people engaged in political activity rely on what Abraham Kaplan calls "logic-in-use"; political science in any form uses a "reconstructed logic."[8] Logic-in-use tends to be oriented toward problem solving, has a severely limited time horizon, and operates in the context of ambiguity, contingency, conflict, and ignorance. On the other hand, political science tends to isolate questions or problems in ways that those engaged in politics cannot do, imposes an orderliness and consistency that is usually not possible in day-to-day life, and can eliminate the distractions of conflict. Political science in general, including political theory, abstracts itself from the logic and reasoning used by those people who are engaged in politics. It then attempts, through systematic study, to clarify the events, actions, motives, and implications of the political process. Political theory is suspicious of the thinking offered by political actors and is always seeking a more adequate, logical explanation—one that can be generalized. Political logic-in-use in general, and political myth in particular, rarely measures up to the factual accuracy demanded by history and empirical political science or to the logical coherence and depth of meaning sought by political theory.

A reconstructed political logic inherently threatens political logic-in-use by calling into question the latter's adequacy. By so doing, political theory, which is a reconstructed logic, threatens to undermine the political myth upon which the political system is built; this is part of the age-old conflict between the polis and political philosophy.

What happens when a self-governing, self-defining people find themselves with a politically active class that is at one and the same time (1) disproportionately influential in the ongoing political process, (2) the primary manipulator and defender of political myth, and (3) the generator of political theory? The resulting tension constantly calls the political myth into question, dilutes political theory, and confuses or conflates myth and theory.

A nation in which there is a coherent elite allows for the possibility that those who largely run the political system can do so based upon a theory that is understood. The elite can use the theory as they alter the political system to meet changing circumstances. The unifying political myth, which the elite control, can be gradually altered to support needed changes in the political system and can be maintained in such a way as to support the political theory. That is, the political myth, which structures the behavior of the many, can be made supportive of the ends of the political theory, which the many do not understand. Elitists often cite this coherence as a strength of elitism.

In the United States, however, although there may be elites, the open, relatively democratic system makes them part of a broader active political class, which is fragmented and fairly porous from below. The inclusion of new members from new groups leads the active political class to alter the unifying political myth accordingly. Yet since political theory is also generated by members of this class, theory is often appropriated for political purposes, sometimes in the service of maintaining or altering the myth, sometimes in the service of undermining the myth. The conflation of theory and myth simply worsens the confusion between theory and ideology. It also has the often unrecognized effect of injecting into a consensual political myth the logical imperative of theory, which too often results in a politics of perfectionism or fanaticism.

Fanaticism is, at its heart, the attempt to create perfection on earth, to eradicate the illogical or the imperfect or both. Part of the task assigned to American political theory is to remind us of the difference between a theory that explains political actions and the logic-in-use that produces political action. The ability to distinguish the two, to use theory to advance political reasoning without collapsing one into the other, defines the peculiar mental discipline of American political theory. It is a discipline sorely needed by a system of popular control, in which the active political class has a double role and is large, diverse, and open.

Those of us who pursue American political theory must attempt to be rational and objective, but we must also try to be responsible. Responsibility entails maintaining a constant vigil against the imperfections of the political logic-in-use, but it also means avoiding the destruction of that common logic, whether by undermining the shared political myth completely or by destroying the morale of those people who must use political logic to achieve the ends needed for the common good.

Finally, if American political theory is to become whole again, we will need to ignore those people who cannot resist the more extreme forms of the natural human inclination to think that whatever they do is the most important or the only activity worth pursuing. There are issues that separate students of American politics and theory, and these issues are real enough and important enough for us to treat them seriously through a continuing discussion, no matter how heated. Perhaps the one quality most needed for our discipline to thrive, the last element in a successful preface, is a continued dedication to truth in its various guises, coupled with humility.

Appendix: European Works Read and Cited by the American Founding Generation

Addison, Joseph (1672–1719). *The Freeholder; Or Political Essays*. London, 1716.

———. *Miscellaneous Works*. London, 1721.

d'Alambert, Jean (1717–1783), and Denis Diderot (1713–1784). *Encyclopedia*. Paris, 1751–1765.

Anderson, Adam (1692–1767). *Historical and Chronological Deduction of the Origin of Commerce*. London, 1764.

Aristotle (384–322 B.C.). *Nichomachean Ethics*.

———. *Politics*.

Ashley, Anthony (third earl of Shaftesbury, 1671–1713). *Characteristics of Men, Manners, Opinions, and Times*. London, 1711.

Atwood, William (d. ca. 1705). *The Fundamental Constitution of the English Government*. London, 1690.

Bacon, Francis (1561–1626). *The Advancement of Learning*. London, 1605.

———. *Novum Organum*. London, 1620.

———. *De Argumentis scientiarum*. London, 1623.

———. *Essays*. London, 1625.

———. *The New Atlantis*. London, 1627.

Bacon, Nathaniel (1593–1660). *An Historical Discourse of the Uniformity of the Government of England*. London, 1647–1651.

Barrington, Daines (1727–1800). *Observations upon the Statutes, Chiefly the more Ancient, from the Magna Carta to the 21st of James I*. London, 1766.

Beattie, James (1735–1803). *Essays on the Nature and Immutability of Truth*. Edinburgh, 1770.

———. *Dissertations, Moral and Critical*. London, 1783.

Beccaria, Cesare (1738–1794). *An Essay on Crimes and Punishments*. Livorno, 1764.

Berkeley, George (1685–1753). *Treatise Concerning the Principles of Human Knowledge*. London, 1710.

Blackstone, William (1723–1780). *Commentaries on the Laws of England*. 4 vols. Oxford, 1765–1769.

Blair, Hugh (1718–1800). *Sermons*. Edinburgh, 1777.

Bolingbroke, Henry St. John, Viscount (1678–1751). *The Freeholder's Political Catechism*. London, 1733.

159

_____. *A Dissertation upon Parties*. London, 1735.

_____. *Remarks on the History of England*. London, 1743.

_____. *The Idea of a Patriot King*. London, 1749.

_____. *A Letter on the Spirit of Patriotism*. London, 1749.

_____. *Letters on the Study and Use of History*. London, 1752.

Boyle, Robert (1627–1691). *The Sceptical Chymist*. London, 1682.

Burgh, James (1714–1775). *Britain's Remembrancer*. London, 1746.

_____. *Political Disquisitions*. London, 1774–1775.

Burlamaqui, Jean Jacques (1694–1748). *The Principles of Natural Law*. London, 1748.

Butler, Joseph (1692–1752). *The Analogy of Religion, Natural and Revealed*. London, 1736.

Care, Henry (1646–1688). *English Liberties*. London, 1682.

Child, Josiah (1630–1699). *A New Discourse of Trade*. London, 1690.

Cicero (106–43 B.C.). *De Legibus*.

_____. *De Officis*.

_____. *De Oratione*.

_____. *De Republica*.

Clarendon, Earl of. See Edward Hyde.

Clarke, Samuel (1675–1729). *A Discourse Concerning the Being and Attributes of God*. London, 1705.

Coke, Edward (1552–1634). *Institutes of the Laws of England*. 4 vols. London, 1628–1644.

Contarini, Gasparo (1484–1542). *The Commonwealth and Government of Venice*. Venice, 1544 and London, 1599.

Davenant, Charles (1656–1714). *An Essay upon Ways and Means*. London, 1695.

_____. *An Essay on the East-India Trade*. London, 1696.

Davies, John (1569–1626). *Report of Cases and Matters in Law, Resolved and Adjudged in the King's Court in Ireland*. London, 1615.

Defoe, Daniel (1661–1731). *An Essay upon Projects*. London, 1697.

_____. *True-Born Englishman*. London, 1701.

_____. *Robinson Crusoe*. London, 1719.

_____. *A Plan for English Commerce*. London, 1728.

Delolme, Jean Louis (1740–1805). *The Constitution of England*. Amsterdam, 1771.

Demosthenes (384?–322 B.C.). *Philippics*. 351, 344, and 341 B.C.

Denham, James Steuart (1712–1780). *An Inquiry into the Principles of Political Economy*. London, 1767.

Descartes, Rene (1596–1650). *Discourse on Method*. 1637.

_____. *Meditations de prima philosophia*. 1641.

_____. *Principia philosophiae*. 1644.

_____. *Traite des passions de l'ame*. 1650.

Diderot. See d'Alambert.

Doddridge, Philip (1702–1751). *The Rise and Progress of Religion in the Soul*. London, 1745.

Dunbar, James (?–1798). *Essays on the History of Mankind in Rude and Uncultivated Ages*. London, 1780.

Falconer, William (1744–1824). *Remarks on the Influence of Climate, Situation, Nature of Country, Population, &c. upon Mankind*. London, 1781.

Ferguson, Adam (1723-1816). *Essay on the History of Civil Society*. London, 1771.

Fortescue, John (1394-1476?). *De Laudibus Legum Angliae*. London, 1616.

Gay, John (1685-1732). *Polly*. London, 1729.

_____. *Fables*. London, 1727-1738.

Goldsmith, Oliver (1728-1774). *Roman History*. 2 vols. London, 1769.

_____. *The History of England*. 4 vols. London, 1774.

Grotius, Hugo de (1583-1645). *De Jure Belli ac Pacis libri tres*. London, 1625.

Guicciardini, Francesco (1483-1540). *The History of Italy*. Florence, 1561.

Guthrie, William (1708-1770). *General History of England*. London, 1744-1751.

Hale, Mathew (1609-1676). *The History of the Common Law of England*. London, 1713.

Harrington, James (1611-1677). *Oceana*. London, 1656.

Harvey, William (1578-1657). *On the Movement of the Heart and Blood in Animals*. London, 1628.

Hawkins, William (1673-1746). *A Treatise of the Pleas of the Crown*. London, 1739.

Helvetius, Claude Adrien (1715-1771). *A Treatise on Man*. Paris, 1772.

Hoadley, Bishop Benjamin (1676-1761). *The Origin and Institute of Civil Government*. London, 1709.

Hobbes, Thomas (1588-1678). *Leviathan*. London, 1651.

Home, Henry (Lord Kames, 1696-1782). *Essays on the Principles of Morality and Natural Religion*. Edinburgh, 1751.

_____. *Historical Law Tracts*. Edinburgh, 1761.

_____. *Sketches of the History of Man*. Edinburgh, 1774.

Hooker, Richard (1554-1600). *Laws of Ecclesiastical Polity*. 4 vols. London, 1593-1597.

Hulme, Obadiah (d. 1791). *An Historical Essay on the English Constitution*. London, 1771.

Hume, David (1711-1776). *Treatise of Human Nature*. London, 1739-1740.

_____. *An Inquiry Concerning Human Understanding*. London, 1748.

_____. *Treatise: An Enquiry Concerning the Principles of Morals*. London, 1751.

_____. *Political Discourses*. London, 1752.

_____. *History of England*. London, 1754-1762.

_____. *The Natural History of Religion*. London, 1755.

_____. *Dialogues Concerning Natural Religion*. London, 1779.

Hutcheson, Francis (1694-1746). *Inquiry into the Original of Our Ideas of Beauty and Virtue*. London, 1725.

_____. *Essay on the Nature and Conduct of the Passions and Affections*. London, 1728.

_____. *Short Introduction to Moral Philosophy*. Glasgow, 1747.

_____. *A System of Moral Philosophy*. London, 1755.

Hyde, Edward (first earl of Clarendon, 1609-1674). *History of the Rebellion and Civil Wars of England*. Oxford, 1702.

Kames, Lord. See Home, Henry.

Law, John (1671-1729). *Money and Trade Considered*. Edinburgh, 1705.

Livy (Titus Livius, 59 B.C.-A.D. 17). *History of Rome*.

Locke, John (1632-1704). *An Essay Concerning Human Understanding*. London, 1690.

_____. *Two Treatises on Government*. London, 1690.

_____. *First Letter on Toleration*. The first of three published in various forms individually and together in the 1690s.

_____. *Some Considerations of the Consequences of the Lowering of Interest and Raising the Value of Money*. London, 1691.

_____. *On the Reasonableness of Christianity*. London, 1696.

Lyttelton, George Lord (1709–1773). *Letters from a Persian in England to a Friend at Ispahan*. London, 1735.

_____. *Considerations upon the Present State of Affairs at Home and Abroad*. London, 1739.

Mably, Abbe Gabriel (1709–1785). *Observations on the Romans*. Paris, 1740.

_____. *Observations on the Government and Laws of the United States*. Amsterdam, 1784.

Macaulay, Catharine (1731–1791). *History of England*. 8 vols. London, 1763–1783.

Machiavelli, Niccolo (1469–1527). *Discourses on the First Ten Books of Livy*. Rome, 1531.

_____. *The Prince*. Florence, 1532.

Mariana, Juan de (1536?–1623?). *De rege et regis Institutione*. N.p., n.d.

_____. *Historiae de rebus Hispaniae*. N.p., n.d.

Millar, John (1735–1801). *Observations Concerning the Distinctions of Ranks and Society*. London, 1771.

_____. *An Historical View of the English Government*. London, 1787.

Milton, John (1608–1674). *The Ready and Easy Way to Establish a Free Commonwealth*. London, 1660.

Molesworth, Robert (1656–1725). *An Account of Denmark as It Was in the Year 1692*. London, 1694.

Montagu, Edward W. (1713–1776). *Reflections on the Rise and Fall of the Antient Republicks Adapted to the Present State of Great Britain*. London, 1759.

Montesquieu, Charles Louis de Secondat, Baron (1689–1755). *Persian Letters*. Paris, 1734.

_____. *Reflections on the Causes of the Rise and Fall of the Roman Empire*. Paris, 1734.

_____. *The Spirit of the Laws*. Paris, 1748.

Moyle, Walter (1672–1721), and John Trenchard (1662–1723). *A Short History of Standing Armies in England*. London, 1698.

_____. *The Whole Works*. London, 1727.

Neville, Henry (1620–1694). *Plato Redivivus; Or a Dialogue Concerning Government*. London, 1681.

Newton, Isaac (1642–1727). *Philosophiae naturalis Principia mathematica*. London, 1687.

North, Dudley (1641–1691). *Discourses upon Trade*. London, 1691.

Paley, William (1743–1805). *Principles of Moral and Political Philosophy*. London, 1785.

Petty, William (1623–1686). *Five Essays in Political Arithmetic*. London, 1687.

Petyt, William (1636–1707). *The Antient Right of the Commons of England Asserted*. London, 1680.

Plutarch (46–120). *Roman Lives*.

Polybius (210–122 B.C.). James Hampton, ed., *The General History of Polybius*. 2 vols. London, 1762–1763.

Pope, Alexander (1688–1744). *The Dunciad*. London, 1728.

_____. *Of False Taste: An Epistle . . . to Lord Burlington*. London, 1731.

_____. *Of the Use of Riches: An Epistle . . . to Lord Bathurst*. London, 1732.

_____. *An Essay on Man*. London, 1733–1734.

Pownall, Thomas (1722–1805). *Principles of Polity: Being the Grounds and Reasons of Civil Empire*. London, 1752.

Price, Richard (1723–1791). *Observations on the Nature of Civil Liberty*. London, 1776.

_____. *Observations on the Importance of the American Revolution*. London, 1784.

Priestley, Joseph (1733–1804). *Essay on the First Principles of Government*. London, 1768.

Pufendorf, Samuel, Baron von (1632–1694). *Elementa Jurisprudentiae universalis*. Frankfurt, 1661.

_____. *De Jure naturae et gentium*. Frankfurt, 1672.

Ralph, James (1705–1762). *History of England during the Reigns of King William, Queen Anne, and King George I*. London, 1744–1746.

Rapin-Thoyras, Paul de (1661–1725). *History of England*. 15 vols. London, 1726–1731.

Raynal, Abbe Guillaume Thomas Francois (1713–1796). *Philosophical and Political History of the Settlements and Trade of the Europeans in the East and West Indies*. Amsterdam, 1770.

Reid, Thomas (1710–1796). *An Inquiry into the Human Mind*. London, 1764.

_____. *Essays on the Intellectual Powers of Man*. Edinburgh, 1785.

Robertson, William (1721–1793). *History of Scotland*. London, 1759.

_____. *History of the Reign of the Emperor Charles V*. London, 1769.

_____. *History of America*. London, 1777.

Rollin, Charles (1661–1741). *The Ancient History*. 2 vols. London, 1739–1750.

Rousseau, Jean Jacques (1712–1778). *Discours sur l'origine de l'inégalité des hommes*. Geneva, 1754.

_____. *Contrat social*. Geneva, 1762.

_____. *Emile*. Geneva, 1762.

Rutherforth, Thomas (1712–1771). *Institutes of Natural Law*. London, 1754.

Shaftesbury, Earl of. See Ashley, Anthony.

Sidney, Algernon (1622–1683). *Discourses Concerning Government*. London, 1698.

Smith, Adam (1723–1790). *Theory of Moral Sentiments*. Edinburgh, 1759.

_____. *Inquiry into the Nature and Causes of the Wealth of Nations*. London, 1776.

Somers, John (1651–1716). *Vox populi, Vox dei: Judgement of Kingdoms and Nations Concerning the Rights, Privileges, and Properties of the People*. London, 1709.

Stuart, Gilbert (1742–1786). *View of Society in Europe in Its Progress from Rudeness to Refinement*. Edinburgh, 1778.

Suarez, Francisco (1548–1617). *De Defensione fidei*. N.p., n.d.

_____. *Tractatus de legibus*. N.p., n.d.

Sullivan, Francis Stoughton (1719–1776). *An Historical Treatise of the Feudal Law and the Constitution and Laws of England*. London, 1772.

Swift, Jonathan (1667–1745). *Discourse on the Contests and Dissensions between the Nobles and Commons in Athens and Rome*. London, 1701.

_____. *Gulliver's Travels*. London, 1726.

Swift, Jonathan (1667–1745), ed. *The Works of Sir William Temple*. 2 vols. London, 1750.

Tacitus (55–120). *Germania*.

————. *Histories*.

Temple, William (1628–1699). *Works*. *See* Swift, Jonathan, ed.

————. *Observations Upon the United Provinces of the Netherlands*. London, 1673.

————. *Essay Upon the Origin and Nature of Government*. London, 1680.

Thucydides, (460?–400? B.C.). *The History of the Peloponnesian War*.

Tillotson, John (1630–1694). *Sermons*. 8 vols. London, 1671–1684.

Tindal, Matthew. *See* Tyndale.

Toland, John (1660–1722). *Christianity Not Mysterious*. London, 1696.

————. *The State Anatomy of Great Britain*. London, 1717.

Trenchard, John (1662–1723), and Thomas Gordon (?–1750). *Cato's Letters*. London, 1724.

Tyndal, Matthew (1653–1733). *Christianity as Old as Creation*. London, 1730.

Vattel, Emmerich de (1714–1767). *The Law of Nations*. London, 1759–1760.

Voltaire, Francois Arouet de (1694–1778). *Letters on the English Nation*. London, 1733.

————. *Works*. Paris, 1751.

————. *General History and State of Europe*. Geneva, 1756.

Whitelocke, Bulstrode (1605–1674). *Memorials of the English Affairs; Or, an Historical Account of What Passed from the Beginning of the Reign of King Charles the First, to the King Charles the Second his Happy Restoration*. London, 1682.

Wollaston, William (1660–1724). *The Religion of Nature Delineated*. London, 1722.

Notes

Chapter One: What Is American Political Theory?

1. Richard Henry Tawney, *The Acquisitive Society* (New York: Harcourt and Brace, 1920), 108.

2. For a discussion of the profession's early years see David M. Ricci, *The Tragedy of Political Science: Politics, Scholarship, and Democracy* (New Haven, Conn.: Yale University Press, 1984), ch. 3.

3. *The American Political Science Association Membership Directory*, published yearly by the association in Washington, D.C. See, for example, the "Classification of Members by Fields of Interest" in the table of contents.

4. See any issue of the *APSA Personnel Service Newsletter* published monthly by the American Political Science Association in Washington, D.C.—especially the September through December issues.

5. Good examples of the first are Kenneth M. Dolbeare, ed., *American Political Thought* (Monterey, Calif.: Duxbury Press, 1985), and Michael B. Levy, ed., *Political Thought in America: An Anthology*, 2d ed. (Chicago: Dorsey Press, 1988). Examples of the second are A. J. Beitzinger, *A History of American Political Thought* (New York: Harper and Row, 1972), and Max J. Skidmore, *American Political Thought* (New York: St. Martin's Press, 1978).

6. A good example is Leon P. Baradat, *Political Ideologies: Their Origins and Impact*, 4th ed. (Englewood Cliffs, N.J.: Prentice-Hall, 1991), esp. 6–10. His usage is fairly typical but unusual in the depth to which the position is explored.

7. See, for example, Angus Campbell et al., *The American Voter* (New York: John Wiley and Sons, 1960).

8. Robert E. Lane, *Political Ideology: Why the Common Man Believes What He Does* (New York: Free Press, 1962). A major precursor to Lane was Harold D. Lasswell, whose major works included *Power and Personality* (New York: Viking Press, 1948) and *Psychopathology and Politics* (New York: Viking Press, 1960).

9. The examples are legion, but a clear statement of the view can be found in Alan C. Isaak, *Scope and Methods of Political Science: An Introduction to the Methodology of Political Inquiry* (Homewood, Ill.: Dorsey Press, 1969), 4.

10. For an overview and discussion of critical theory see Richard J. Bernstein, *The Restructuring of Social and Political Theory* (New York: Harcourt Brace

Jovanovich, 1976), Part 4. Those familiar with Bernstein's work will recognize that even though a different vocabulary is being used, the position argued in this chapter is very similar to Bernstein's.

11. See, for example, Albert Somit and Joseph Tannenhaus, *The Development of American Political Science: From Burgess to Behavioralism* (Boston: Allyn and Bacon, 1967), 24.

12. Frank J. Goodnow, "The Work of the American Political Science Association," *Proceedings* 1 (1904): 35.

13. See, for example, George J. Graham, Jr., *Methodological Foundations for Political Analysis* (Waltham, Mass.: Xerox College Publishing, 1971), 20–22.

14. Both quotes are from E. E. Schattschneider, *Two Hundred Million Americans in Search of a Government* (New York: Holt, Rinehart and Winston, 1969), 8.

15. Most of these definitions are derived from discussions by Isaak, *Scope and Methods of Political Science*, ch. 2, and Ricci, *Tragedy of Political Science*, ch. 7.

16. Charles S. Hyneman, *The Study of Politics* (Urbana: University of Illinois Press, 1956), 26.

17. Alfred de Grazia, *Political Behavior* (New York: Free Press, 1965), 24.

18. Harold Lasswell and Abraham Kaplan, *Power and Society: A Framework for Political Inquiry* (New Haven, Conn.: Yale University Press, 1950), 75, 85.

19. William Bluhm, *Theories of the Political System* (Englewood Cliffs, N.J.: Prentice-Hall, 1965), 5.

20. David Easton, *The Political System: An Inquiry into the State of Political Science*, 2d ed. (New York: Knopf, 1971), 143–44.

21. The definition of power used here is taken from Robert A. Dahl, "The Concept of Power," *Behavioral Science* 2:3 (July 1957): 201–15 (see 203).

22. Isaak, *Scope and Methods of Political Science*, 25.

23. See Aristotle, *Nichomachean Ethics*, tr. David Ross (New York: Oxford University Press, 1990), esp. Book 10, and Christian Bay, "Politics and Pseudo-Politics: A Critical Evaluation of Some Behavioral Literature," *American Political Science Review* 59:1 (March 1965): 39–51.

24. David W. Minar, *Ideas and Politics: The American Experience* (Homewood, Ill.: Dorsey Press, 1964), 97.

25. Donald S. Lutz, *The Origins of American Constitutionalism* (Baton Rouge: Louisiana State University Press, 1988), 13–16.

26. There are distressingly few efforts to blend the empirical and theoretical for purposes of predicting institutional consequences. An especially good example of the argument here is Douglas Rae's *The Political Consequences of Electoral Laws* (New Haven, Conn.: Yale University Press, 1967).

27. Again, there are very few examples to which we can point. One might be Christian Bay's *The Structure of Freedom* (Stanford, Calif.: Stanford University Press, 1970). Another might be Jeanne N. Knutson's *The Human Basis of the Polity* (Chicago: Aldine/Atherton, 1972). Neither of these deals with American political theory, but both attempt to clean up the literature in political psychology in a search for theoretical propositions.

28. The idea of a science of politics certainly can be found in the writing of Europeans such as Francis Bacon, David Hume, and Baron de Montesquieu, but the receptiveness of twentieth-century American political science

to empirical, statistical, and science-imitating approaches cannot be explained by the presence of these ideas among European thinkers.

29. *The Federalist* by Alexander Hamilton, James Madison, and John Jay is often considered our greatest political text, but as we will see in the next chapter it is an assembled text, not one written as a piece as Tocqueville's work was, and thus is handicapped when compared to the great European thinkers. John C. Calhoun's *Disquisition on Government* is not an assembled text, but its depth suffers from its brevity. Herbert Croly's *The Promise of American Life* physically resembles a great text but is too particularistic to be so categorized. Other candidates spring to mind, but they are not read by anyone; thus Hamilton and Madison, Tocqueville, Calhoun, and Croly would seem to have written the most recognized theoretical texts we have.

Chapter Two: American Political Texts and Their Analysis

1. See, for example, Leo Strauss, *Persecution and the Art of Writing* (Chicago: University of Chicago Press, 1952).

2. For a detailed development of this position see Donald S. Lutz, *The Origins of American Constitutionalism* (Baton Rouge: Louisiana State University Press, 1988).

3. The position being developed in this section is my own, but a significant debt is owed to the work of others whose interesting and sensible analysis is particularly appreciated. See, for example, Wayne C. Booth, *A Rhetoric of Irony* (Chicago: University of Chicago Press, 1975); E. D. Hirsch, Jr., *The Aims of Interpretation* (Chicago: University of Chicago Press, 1976); Wolfgang Iser, *The Act of Reading* (Baltimore, Md.: Johns Hopkins University Press, 1978); Frank Kermode, *The Genesis of Secrecy* (Cambridge, Mass.: Harvard University Press, 1979); Paul Ricoeur, *Interpretation Theory: Discourse and the Surplus of Meaning* (Fort Worth: Texas Christian University Press, 1976); Walter J. Slatoff, *With Respect to Readers* (Ithaca, N.Y.: Cornell University Press, 1970); and Conal Condren, *The Status and Appraisal of Classic Texts: An Essay on Political Theory, Its Inheritance, and the History of Ideas* (Princeton, N.J.: Princeton University Press, 1985).

4. Hanna Fenichel Pitkin, *The Concept of Representation* (Berkeley: University of California Press, 1967).

5. William Shakespeare, *The Merchant of Venice*, Act 2, scene 1, and Sir Walter Scott, *Redgauntlet* (Edinburgh: Constable, 1824), ch. 11.

6. Terence Ball and J.G.A. Pocock have edited and contributed to an important book that provides interesting and telling examples from the history of American political theory. See their *Conceptual Change and the Constitution* (Lawrence: University Press of Kansas, 1988).

7. For a discussion indicating that "common good" meant precisely this in eighteenth-century America see Lutz, *Origins of American Constitutionalism*, esp. 28–30, 76–77, and 89–90.

8. For an accessible discussion of cognitive psychology see the book from which this example was taken—Morton Hunt, *The Universe Within: A New Science Explores the Human Mind* (New York: Simon and Schuster, 1982).

9. See Bernard Bailyn, ed., *Pamphlets of the American Revolution* (Cambridge, Mass.: Belknap Press, 1967), and Herbert Storing, ed., *The Complete*

Antifederalist, 7 vols. (Chicago: University of Chicago Press, 1981). Storing went further and suggested a list of pamphlets written by other Federalists that should be collected to supplement the collected essays by Hamilton, Madison, and Jay, but he died before he could publish them. See Herbert Storing, "The 'Other' Federalist Papers: A Preliminary Sketch," *Political Science Reviewer* 6 (1976): 215–47. A listing of other assembled texts published before 1983 can be found in Charles S. Hyneman and Donald S. Lutz, *American Political Writing during the Founding Era, 1760–1805,* 2 vols. (Indianapolis: Liberty Press, 1983), 1:392–93, as well as an annotated bibliography of more than five hundred items beyond the seventy-five published in this collection. The highly regarded collection edited by Philip B. Kurland and Ralph Lerner, *The Founders' Constitution,* 5 vols. (Chicago: University of Chicago Press, 1987), also proceeds on the premise of assembled texts.

Chapter Three: Toward a Complete Text on the Bill of Rights

1. I have relied upon the texts as found in Richard L. Perry, ed., *Sources of Our Liberties* (New York: Associated College Presses for the American Bar Association, 1959), 11–22, 73–75, and 245–50.
2. See, for example, ibid., pp. 23–24. For a lucid description of the development of English common law in general and the position of Magna Carta in particular, see Arthur R. Hogue, *Origins of the Common Law* (Indianapolis: Liberty Press/Liberty Classics, 1988), and also T. F. Plucknett, *A Concise History of the Common Law* (Boston: Little, Brown, 1956).
3. See Bernard Schwartz, *The Great Rights of Mankind: A History of the Bill of Rights* (New York: Oxford University Press, 1977), p. 197; Irving Brant, *The Bill of Rights: Its Origin and Meaning* (Indianapolis: Bobbs-Merrill Company, 1965), esp. chs. 5 and 6; William Nelson, *The Americanization of the Common Law: The Impact of Legal Change on Massachusetts Society, 1760–1830* (Cambridge, Mass.: Harvard University Press, 1975); Jack P. Greene, *Peripheries and Center: Constitutional Development in the Extended Politics of the British Empire and the United States, 1607–1788* (Athens: University of Georgia Press, 1986); and Shannon C. Stimson, *The American Revolution in the Law* (Princeton, N.J.: Princeton University Press, 1990).
4. *Annals of Congress,*12 vols. (Philadelphia, 1804), 1: 436.
5. The most accurate and accessible source for these ratifying convention records is Merrill Jensen, John P. Kaminski, Gaspare J. Saladino et al., eds., *The Documentary History of the Ratification of the Constitution* (Madison: University of Wisconsin Press, 1976–).
6. The state constitutions and their respective state bills of rights can be found in Francis N. Thorpe, ed., *The Federal and State Constitutions,* 7 vols. (Washington, D.C.: Government Printing Office, 1907), and also in William F. Swindler, ed., *Sources and Documents of the United States Constitutions,* 10 vols. (Dobbs Ferry, N.Y.: Oceana Publications, 1973–1979). Swindler published a second series of three volumes in 1982 that contains documents relating to the national Constitution.
7. Thorpe, *Constitutions* (Maryland), 1686–91, (Massachusetts), 1889–93, and (New Hampshire), 2453–57.
8. Ibid. (Virginia), 3812–14, and (Pennsylvania), 3082–84.

9. These documents are widely scattered, but many can be found in the two series of volumes by Swindler cited in n. 6 as well as in Thorpe. Those not found in these volumes may be located in Donald S. Lutz, *Documents of Political Foundation Written by Colonial Americans* (Philadelphia: ISHI Press, 1986).

10. See Lutz, *Documents of Political Foundation,* 435–42, 403–10, 359–62, 309–14, 255–302, and 189–94.

11. The argument being made here is fully developed in Donald S. Lutz, *The Origins of American Constitutionalism* (Baton Rouge: Louisiana State University Press, 1988).

12. There is a distinctively Protestant quality to the sort of religiosity that is here being summarized. To pursue further the relationship of religion to American political theory see Ellis Sandoz, *A Government of Laws: Political Theory, Religion, and the American Founding* (Baton Rouge: Louisiana State University Press, 1990); J. W. Smith and A. L. Jameson, *Religion in American Life,* 4 vols. (Princeton, N.J.: Princeton University Press, 1961); Anson Phelps Stokes, ed., *Church and State and the U.S.* (New York: Harper and Row, 1950); Cushing Strout, *The New Heavens and New Earth: Political Religion in America* (New York: Harper and Row, 1974); E. Brooks Holifield, *The Covenant Sealed: The Development of Puritan Sacramental Theology in Old and New England, 1570–1720* (New Haven, Conn.: Yale University Press, 1974); and Lutz, *Origins of American Constitutionalism,* chs. 2 and 3.

13. It is not easy to study English common law directly in America; the mass of original documents is not available even in the best American libraries. The main secondary source used by colonists was Edward Coke, *Institutes of the Laws of England,* 4 vols., originally published in London between 1628 and 1644 and now available in most libraries in one of its reprinted versions. Otherwise see James C. Holt, ed., *Magna Carta and the Idea of Liberty* (Malabar, Fla.: Robert E. Krieger Publishing Company, 1982); J. C. Holt, *Magna Carta* (Cambridge: Cambridge University Press, 1965); Stephen D. White, *Sir Edward Coke and "The Grievances of the Commonwealth," 1621–1628* (Chapel Hill: University of North Carolina Press, 1979); Arthur R. Hogue, *Origins of the Common Law* (Indianapolis: Liberty Press/Liberty Classics, 1988); and J. W. Gough, *Fundamental Law in English Constitutional History* (Oxford: Oxford University Press, 1961).

14. These documents can be found in varying combinations in the volumes cited in n. 9.

15. Thorpe, *Constitutions* (North Carolina), 2788.

16. Ibid. (Maryland), 1687.

17. Ibid. (Massachusetts), 1891.

18. Ibid. (Pennsylvania), 3083

19. John Phillip Reid, *The Concept of Liberty in the Age of the American Revolution* (Chicago: University of Chicago Press, 1988). See also the work of J. C. Holt cited in n. 13.

20. Thorpe, *Constitutions* (Pennsylvania), 3082.

21. Ibid. (Massachusetts), 1889.

22. Ibid. (Pennsylvania), 3082.

23. Ibid. (Massachusetts), 1889.

24. Algernon Sidney, a contemporary of John Locke and in the same political faction, was tried and executed in 1683 for treason against the king. His

conviction was based on his writings in an unpublished manuscript entitled *Discourses on Government*, which laid out the case for popular sovereignty, representative government, and natural rights. Published in London in 1698, the book had considerable overlap with Locke's *Second Treatise on Government*, and in revolutionary America the two men were frequently referred to as theoretically interchangeable. In fact, Sidney was the more radical of the two. Locke supported legislative supremacy, but Sidney defended the more radical popular-sovereignty position in language that was closer to American views. Sidney's book has been most recently reprinted (1990) by Liberty Press/Liberty Classics of Indianapolis.

25. See Alexander Hamilton, John Jay, and James Madison, *The Federalist* (Indianapolis: Modern library, 1937), 555–61.

26. These and other documents can be found in various combinations in the previously cited volumes by Thorpe, Swindler, and Jensen et al. and in Lutz (*Documents*).

27. The position is more fully developed in Lutz, *Origins of American Constitutionalism*. A detailed analysis of the rise of individualism in American political and legal thought and the implications of this change for our political system can be found in Lawrence M. Friedman, *The Republic of Choice: Law, Authority, and Culture* (Cambridge, Mass.: Harvard University Press, 1990).

28. For an extended and interesting discussion on this point see Akhil Reed Amar, "The Bill of Rights as a Constitution," *Yale Law Journal* 100 (1990): 1111–90.

29. The approach used here, although somewhat different, is derived from Judith Jarvis Thomson, *The Realm of Rights* (Cambridge, Mass.: Harvard University Press, 1990).

30. For a good introduction to the growing literature on this topic see John Kincaid, "State Court Protections of Individual Rights under State Constitutions: The New Judicial Federalism," *Journal of State Government* 61 (Sept./Oct. 1988): 163–69.

31. For further discussion on this point see Donald S. Lutz, "Protection of Political Participation in Eighteenth Century America," *Albany Law Review* 53:2 (Winter 1989): 327–55.

Chapter Four: Use of History in American Political Theory

1. Benjamin Barber nicely summarizes the antipolitical inclination of modern philosophy, and thus of contemporary political philosophy, in his *Conquest of Politics: Liberal Philosophy in Democratic Times* (Princeton, N.J.: Princeton University Press, 1988). The indifference (at best) of philosophy to political philosophy is exemplified by Hao Wang's summary of contemporary philosophy, in which political philosophy is mentioned only four times, and the fourth mention is dry, terse, and dismissive—"political philosophy, an area not in the center of current academic philosophy." See Hao Wang, *Beyond Analytic Philosophy* (Cambridge, Mass.: MIT Press, 1988), 210.

2. See, for example, Judith Jarvis Thomson, *The Realm of Rights* (Cambridge, Mass.: Harvard University Press, 1990). Although in many ways typical of the philosophical literature, it is also among the best of its kind.

3. Andrew C. McLaughlin, *Foundations of American Constitutionalism*

(New York: New York University Press, 1932), and Charles M. Andrews, *The Colonial Period of American History* (New Haven, Conn.: Yale University Press, 1936).

4. Frederick Jackson Turner did not publish much during his lifetime, and his famous thesis was presented in a paper entitled "The Significance of the Frontier in American History" at the 1893 annual meeting of the American Historical Association. Charles Beard's most influential work was *An Economic Interpretation of the Constitution of the United States* (New York: Macmillan, 1913), and Vernon L. Parrington is best known for *Main Currents in American Thought*, 3 vols. (New York: Harcourt, Brace, 1927-1930).

5. See Robert E. Brown, *Charles Beard and the Constitution: A Critical Analysis of "An Economic Interpretation of the Constitution"* (Princeton, N.J.: Princeton University Press, 1956), and Forrest McDonald, *We the People: The Economic Origins of the Constitution* (Chicago: University of Chicago Press, 1958). See also, Lee Benson, *Turner and Beard: American Historical Writing Reconsidered* (New York: Free Press, 1960). The post-Beardian socioeconomic literature is quite large. Interesting and useful examples include Robert E. Brown, *Middle Class Democracy and the Revolution in Massachusetts, 1691-1780* (Ithaca, N.Y.: Cornell University Press, 1955); Van Beck Hall, *Politics without Parties: Massachusetts, 1780-1791* (Pittsburgh: University of Pittsburgh Press, 1972); Jackson Turner Main, *The Social Structure of Revolutionary America* (Princeton, N.J.: Princeton University Press, 1965); and Chilton Williamson, *American Suffrage from Property to Democracy: 1760-1860* (Princeton, N.J.: Princeton University Press, 1968).

6. See, for example, Carl L. Becker, *The Declaration of Independence* (New York: Harcourt, Brace, 1922), and Louis Hartz, *The Liberal Tradition in America* (New York: Harcourt Brace Jovanovich, 1955).

7. For a fuller discussion of the orthodoxy and its demise from a historian's viewpoint see Robert E. Shalhope, "Toward a Republican Synthesis: The Emergence of an Understanding of Republicanism in American Historiography," *William and Mary Quarterly*, 3d ser., 29 (1972): 49-80.

8. Charles McIlwain, *The American Revolution* (New York: Macmillan, 1923); Arthur M. Schlesinger, *New Viewpoints in American History* (New York: Macmillan, 1922); Charles E. Merriam, *A History of American Political Theories* (New York: Macmillan, 1903); Max Farrand, *The Framing of the Constitution of the United States* (New Haven, Conn.: Yale University Press, 1913); Allan Nevins, *The American States during and after the Revolution, 1775-1789* (New York: Macmillan, 1924); and Merrill Jensen, *The Articles of Confederation* (Madison: University of Wisconsin Press, 1940).

9. Max Farrand, ed., *The Records of the Federal Convention of 1787*, 4 vols. (New Haven, Conn.: Yale University Press, 1937); Jonathan Elliott, ed., *The Debates in the Several State Conventions on the Adoption of the Federal Constitution*, 5 vols. (Philadelphia: J. B. Lippincott, 1901); Paul Leicester Ford, ed., *Pamphlets on the Constitution of the United States* (Brooklyn, N.Y., 1888; reprint, New York: Da Capo Press, 1968); and Francis N. Thorpe, ed., *The Federal and State Constitutions, Colonial Charters, and Other Organic Laws of the United States*, 7 vols. (Washington, D.C.: Government Printing Office, 1907).

10. Parrington, *Main Currents in American Thought*, 286.

11. Edmund S. Morgan, *Inventing the People: The Rise of Popular Sovereignty in England and America* (New York: W. W. Norton, 1988).

12. As distant as the 1940s' perspective seems to us now, historians and social scientists still have the task of explaining why most of our high school texts today use the Beard/Locke approach as their primary explanation for the genesis of the Constitution. Even a number of college-level texts fail to reflect the impact of the past forty years of scholarship.

13. Caroline Robbins, *The Eighteenth Century Commonwealthman* (Cambridge, Mass.: Harvard University Press, 1959); Clinton Rossiter, *Seedtime of the Republic* (New York: Harcourt Brace and World, 1963); and Douglas Adair, "'That Politics May Be Reduced to a Science': David Hume, James Madison, and the Tenth *Federalist*," *Huntington Library Quarterly* 20:2 (June 1957): 343–60.

14. Caroline Robbins, "Algernon Sidney's *Discourses Concerning Government*: Textbook of Revolution," *William and Mary Quarterly*, 3d ser., 4 (1947): 267–96.

15. See Brown, *Charles Beard*, and McDonald, *We the People*.

16. Richard Hofstadter, *The American Political Tradition and the Men Who Made It* (New York: Alfred A. Knopf, 1948); Daniel J. Boorstin, *The Genius of American Politics* (Chicago: University of Chicago Press, 1953); and Hartz, *Liberal Tradition in America*.

17. The most recent republication of this classic work is Arthur F. Bentley, *The Process of Government*, ed. Peter Odegard (1908; Cambridge, Mass.: Harvard University Press, 1967).

18. The discussion here is based upon Dorothy Ross, *The Origins of American Social Science* (New York: Cambridge University Press, 1991), esp. chs. 8 and 9.

19. Charles E. Merriam, "The Present State of the Study of Politics," *American Political Science Review* 15 (May 1921): esp. 174–77.

20. Joseph A. Schumpeter, *Capitalism, Socialism, and Democracy*, 2d ed. (New York: Harper and Row, 1947).

21. Robert A. Dahl, *A Preface to Democratic Theory* (Chicago: University of Chicago Press, 1956). The book has been in continuous print for thirty-five years now and shows no sign of disappearing. It is one of the few books that one can assume has been read by almost every political scientist alive today, regardless of specialization.

22. Martin Diamond, "Democracy and *The Federalist*: A Reconsideration of the Framers' Intent," *American Political Science Review* 53 (March 1959): 52–68.

23. J.G.A. Pocock, "Machiavelli, Harrington, and English Political Ideologies in the Eighteenth Century," *William and Mary Quarterly* 3d ser., 22 (1965): 549–83; J.G.A. Pocock, *The Machiavellian Moment* (Princeton, N.J.: Princeton University Press, 1975); Bernard Bailyn, *The Ideological Origins of the American Revolution* (Cambridge, Mass.: Belknap Press, 1967); and Gordon S. Wood, *The Creation of the American Republic, 1776–1787* (Chapel Hill: University of North Carolina Press, 1969).

24. Donald S. Lutz, "The Relative Influence of European Writers on Late Eighteenth Century American Political Thought," *American Political Science Review* 78 (March 1984): 189–97.

25. Garry Wills, *Inventing America: Jefferson's Declaration of Independence* (Garden City, N.J.: Doubleday, 1978); D. Lundberg and H. H. May, "The En-

lightened Reader in America," *American Quarterly* 28 (special issue, 1976): 262–93.

26. See, for example, Thomas L. Pangle, *The Spirit of Modern Republicanism: The Moral Vision of the American Founders and the Philosophy of Locke* (Chicago: University of Chicago Press, 1988); Isaac Kramnick, *Republicanism and Bourgeois Radicalism: Political Ideology in Late Eighteenth Century England and America* (Ithaca, N.Y.: Cornell University Press, 1990); and Richard Matthew, "Liberalism, Civic Humanism, and the American Political Tradition," *Journal of Politics* 49:4 (December 1987): 1127–53.

27. The first claim is made by Jefferson himself. See Paul Leicester Ford, ed., *The Writings of Thomas Jefferson*, 10 vols. (New York: G. P. Putnam's Sons, 1904–5), 10: 343–44. The second claim is made by Forrest McDonald, *Novus Ordo Seclorum: The Intellectual Origins of the Constitution* (Lawrence: University Press of Kansas, 1985), 205–9. The third claim was first made by Bernard Schwartz, ed., *The Roots of the Bill of Rights*, 5 vols. (New York: Chelsea House Publishers, 1980), 5:1204–20.

28. See Sidney Verba, Norman H. Nie, and Jae-on Kim, *Participation and Political Equality* (New York: Cambridge University Press, 1978), for a useful comparison of participation in seven nations, including the United States. See also Samuel H. Barnes and Max Kasse et al., *Political Action: Mass Participation in Five Western Democracies* (Beverly Hills, Calif.: Sage, 1979); Giuseppe Di Palma, *Apathy and Participation: Mass Politics in Western Societies* (New York: Free Press, 1970); and Marvin E. Olsen, *Participatory Pluralism: Political Participation and Influence in the United States and Sweden* (Chicago: Nelson-Hall, 1982).

29. The discussion here is based most heavily upon Verba, Nie, and Kim, *Participation in America*; Harry Holloway and John George, *Public Opinion: Coalitions, Elites, and Masses*, 2d ed. (New York: St. Martin's Press, 1986); and James A. Stimson, "The Paradox of Ignorant Voters but Competent Electorate," in Donald S. Lutz and Kent L. Tedin, eds., *Perspectives on American and Texas Politics*, 2d ed. (Dubuque, Iowa: Kendall/Hunt Publishing Company, 1987), ch. 4. See also Lester Milbrath and M. L. Goel, *Political Participation*, 2d ed. (Chicago: Rand McNally, 1977); Mary Crisey Kweit and Robert W. Kweit, *Implementing Citizen Participation in a Bureaucratic Society: A Contingency Approach* (New York: Praeger, 1982); Gerald M. Pomper with Susan S. Lederman, *Elections in America: Control and Influence in Democratic Politics*, 2d ed. (New York: Dodd, Mead, 1980); and Gerald M. Pomper, *Voter's Choice: Varieties of American Electoral Behavior* (New York: Dodd, Mead, 1975).

30. In the order in which they are mentioned these collections are Bernard Bailyn, ed., *Pamphlets of the American Revolution* (Cambridge, Mass.: Belknap Press, 1965); Morton Borden, ed., *The Antifederalist Papers* (East Lansing: Michigan State University Press, 1965); Cecelia Kenyon, ed., *The Antifederalists* (Indianapolis: Bobbs-Merrill, 1966); Jacob E. Cooke, ed., *The Federalist* (Cleveland, Ohio: Meridian Books, 1961); Frederick Rudolph, ed., *Essays on Education in the Early Republic* (Cambridge, Mass.: Belknap Press, 1965); Oscar Handlin and Mary Handlin, eds., *The Popular Sources of Political Authority* (Cambridge, Mass.: Harvard University Press, 1966); and Leonard W. Levy, ed., *Freedom of the Press from Zenger to Jefferson: Early American Libertarian Theories* (Indianapolis: Bobbs-Merrill, 1966). Other collections of documents and pamphlets published by historians include Jack P. Greene, ed., *Settlements to*

Society: 1607–1763 (New York: W. W. Norton, 1975); Merrill Jensen, John P. Kaminski, Gaspare J. Saladino et al., eds., *The Documentary History of the Ratification of the Constitution,* a multivolume effort that is still being expanded (Madison: University of Wisconsin Press, 1976–); Keith W. Kavenaugh, ed., *Foundations of Colonial America: A Documentary History* (New York: Chelsea House, 1973); Merrill Jensen, ed., *Tracts of the American Revolution, 1763–1776* (Indianapolis: Bobbs-Merrill, 1978); and William F. Swindler, ed., *Sources and Documents of the United States Constitutions,* 10 vols. (Dobbs Ferry, N.Y.: Oceana Publications, 1973–1979).

31. Charles S. Hyneman and George W. Carey, eds., *A Second Federalist* (New York: Appleton-Century-Crofts, 1967); Herbert J. Storing, "The 'Other' Federalist Papers," *Political Science Reviewer* 6 (Fall 1976): 215–47; Herbert J. Storing with Murray Dry, eds., *The Complete Antifederalist,* 7 vols. (Chicago: University of Chicago Press, 1981); Charles S. Hyneman and Donald S. Lutz, eds., *American Political Writing during the Founding Era, 1760–1805,* 2 vols. (Indianapolis: Liberty Press, 1983); Philip B. Kurland and Ralph Lerner, eds., *The Founders' Constitution,* 5 vols. (Chicago: University of Chicago Press, 1987). Other collections of relevant materials include Donald S. Lutz, ed., *Documents of Political Foundation Written by Colonial Americans* (Philadelphia: ISHI Press, 1986); Irving Mark and Eugene L. Schwaab, eds., *The Faith of Our Fathers: An Anthology Expressing the Aspirations of the American Common Man, 1790–1860* (New York: Octagon Books, 1976); Saul K. Padover, ed., *The World of the Founding Fathers* (New York: A. S. Barnes, 1977); J. R. Pole, ed., *The Revolution in America, 1754–1788: Documents and Commentaries* (Stanford, Calif.: Stanford University Press, 1970); Ralph A. Rossum and Gary L. McDowell, eds., *The American Founding: Politics, Statesmanship, and the Constitution* (Port Washington, N.Y.: Kennikat Press, 1981); Wilson Smith, ed., *Theories of Education in Early America, 1655–1819* (Indianapolis: Bobbs-Merrill, 1973); Stephen L. Schechter, ed., *Roots of the Republic* (Madison, Wis.: Madison House, 1990); and Schwartz, ed., *Roots of the Bill of Rights.* These supplemented a number of earlier collections, most of which were reprinted during the late 1960s and 1970s, including John Almon, ed., *A Collection of Papers Relative to the Dispute between Great Britain and America, 1764–1775* (New York: Da Capo Press, 1971); Elliott, ed., *Debates in the Several State Conventions on the Adoption of the Federal Constitution;* Farrand, ed., *Records of the Federal Convention of 1787;* Peter Force, ed., *American Archives: Fifth Series, A Documentary History of the United States of America* (Washington, D.C.: n.p., 1848); Ford, ed., *Pamphlets on the Constitution of the United States;* Merrill Jensen, ed., *American Colonial Documents to 1776,* vol. 9 in the multivolume series *English Historical Documents* (New York: Oxford University Press, 1955); John Wingate Thornton, ed., *The Pulpit of the American Revolution* (Boston: Gould and Lincoln, 1860); and Thorpe, ed., *Federal and State Constitutions.*

32. For a fuller discussion of this point see Donald S. Lutz, *The Origins of American Constitutionalism* (Baton Rouge: Louisiana State University Press, 1988), ch. 9.

33. Gordon S. Wood, "The Virtues and Interests," a review of Isaac Kramnick, *Republicanism and Bourgeois Radicalism: Political Ideology in Late Eighteenth Century England and America, New Republic,* Feb. 11, 1991, 32–35 (quote from 34). Wood argued this position earlier, but Michael Kammen made the point with equal force in his *People of Paradox: An Inquiry Concerning the Origins*

of American Civilization (New York: Knopf, 1972). Kammen, in this and later writing, has also been an important contributor to historical analysis using the political class as a focus, although he is more interested in detailing the origin and nature of the shared mental states, or culture, that underlie the attitudes of the political class than he is in detailing the political struggles of that class. These are far from the only historians using such a focus, since recourse to the pamphlet literature and a wider base among original sources have become common over the past two decades, but special note might be made of Jack Greene's work. His *Peripheries and Center: Constitutional Development in the Extended Polities of the British Empire and the United States, 1607–1788* (Athens: University of Georgia Press, 1986) is notable for exploring the fissures within the Anglo-American political class that resulted in a de facto system of federalism in the British imperial constitution prior to 1776.

34. See McDonald, *Novus Ordo Seclorum*, 209. Notably, despite the obvious major differences that distinguished these theories, Americans were justified in also seeing some important areas of commonality—for example, the identification of human nature with the body and its instincts, senses, and passions; a conviction that human beings are in conflict with nature; and a belief that government is a contrivance to achieve human ends.

35. Gordon Wood criticizes Kramnick's book as an example of the tendency to argue anachronistically over which paradigm dominated the founders' thinking, but Wood also points to J.G.A. Pocock as a major offender in this regard (see n. 23 for some of Pocock's major work). However correct Wood may be, one must remember that those scholars engaged in developing theory, during the founding or other eras, may or may not have seen the implications (or even the contradictions) of the categories they used. They may have preferred ambiguities but relied on arguments that—if driven to fundamental assumptions—might give a decisive advantage to one or another of the later interpretations. In this sense, one would have to go beyond the ostensible categories of the logic-in-use during the founding era to understand a position completely. Still, the place to begin is with the logic-in-use, not with some prepackaged European model.

36. Wood, *Creation of the American Republic*, 389.

37. Ibid., 517.

Chapter Five: Intellectual History and the American Founding

1. Locke uses the phrase "pursuit of happiness" several times in ch. 21, book 2 of the *Essay Concerning Human Understanding*, so the term, if not Jefferson's formulation linking it with life and liberty, can be found in Locke. Happiness as the end of government is a proposition that can be traced back to Aristotle, but the modern formulation in Jefferson and the other writers mentioned here—the *pursuit* of happiness—implies that either there is no summum bonum or that it is unattainable. A discussion of the various possible sources of Jefferson's phrase can be found in Herbert Gantner, "Jefferson's 'Pursuit of Happiness' and Some Forgotten Men," *William and Mary Quarterly* 2nd ser., 16 (1936): 558–85.

2. Alexander Hamilton, James Madison, John Jay, *The Federalist*, C. Rossiter, ed. (New York: Mentor, 1961), no. 85, 526–27.

3. A somewhat different but compatible position can be found in Edmund S. Morgan, *Inventing the People: The Rise of Popular Sovereignty in England and America* (New York: W. W. Norton, 1988).

4. H. Trevor Colbourn provides a complete review of this literature in *The Lamp of Experience: Whig History and the Intellectual Origins of the American Revolution* (Chapel Hill: University of North Carolina Press, 1965).

5. The books written by the authors mentioned in the text are listed in the Appendix (see pp. 159–64).

6. For a complete review of this literature, its context, and its impact, see J.G.A. Pocock, *The Machiavellian Moment: Florentine Political Thought and the Atlantic Republican Tradition* (Princeton, N.J.: Princeton University Press, 1975), and Caroline Robbins, *The Eighteenth Century Commonwealthman* (Cambridge, Mass.: Harvard University Press, 1959).

7. Charles Francis Adams, ed., *The Works of John Adams* (New York: Little & Brown, 1852), 4: 415.

8. Ibid., 421.

9. Thomas Jefferson, *Writings of Thomas Jefferson*, 64 vols. (Washington, D.C.: Thomas Jefferson Memorial Association, 1907), 15:19.

10. Hamilton, Madison, and Jay, *Federalist*, no. 39, 243.

11. Even a partial list of the Whigs' writings read by Americans would include John Trenchard and Thomas Gordon, Bishop Benjamin Hoadley, Henry Neville, Viscount Bolingbroke, John Milton, Robert Molesworth, Joseph Priestley, John Somers, George Lyttelton, Alexander Pope, Jonathan Swift, James Harrington, the Earl of Shaftesbury (Anthony Ashley), Richard Hooker, Walter Moyle, John Gay, Richard Price, and James Burgh. The basic definition of the Whig literature is taken from Bernard Bailyn, *The Ideological Origins of the American Revolution* (Cambridge, Mass.: Belknap Press of Harvard, 1967). The best overview of this literature's impact on American political thinking of the period is in Gordon S. Wood, *The Creation of the American Republic* (Chapel Hill: University of North Carolina Press, 1969).

12. See, for example, J. P. Greene, *The Intellectual Heritage of the Constitutional Era: The Delegate's Library* (Philadelphia: Library Company of Philadelphia, 1986).

13. Included among these supporters of Coke were Chief Justice Sir Mathew Hale, William Petyt, Lord John Somers, Daines Barrington, Henry Care, William Atwood, Obadiah Hulme, Francis Stoughton Sullivan, William Hawkins, and the Earl of Clarendon (Edward Hyde). The works of these legal historians were scattered throughout personal and college legal libraries in America.

14. An assessment of the actual availability of certain books in America during the era can be found in D. Lundberg and H. F. May, "The Enlightened Reader in America," *American Quarterly* 28 (special issue, 1976): 262–93.

15. Steven Dworetz's *The Unvarnished Doctrine* (Durham, N.C.: Duke University Press, 1990) demonstrates Locke's importance for the American revolutionary era (see also Table 5.3).

16. R. H. Campbell and A. S. Skinner, eds., *The Origins and Nature of the Scottish Enlightenment* (Edinburgh: John Donald Press, 1982); Istvan Hunt and Michael Ignatieff, eds., *Wealth and Virtue: The Shaping of Political Economy in the Scottish Enlightenment* (Cambridgeshire: Cambridge University Press, 1983);

and Garry Wills, *Inventing America: Jefferson's Declaration of Independence* (New York: Doubleday, 1978).

17. See, e.g., Douglass Adair, "'That Politics May Be Reduced to a Science': David Hume, James Madison, and the Tenth *Federalist*," reprinted in Trevor Colbourn, ed., *Fame and the Founding Fathers: Essays by Douglass Adair* (New York: W. W. Norton, 1974), 93–106.

18. The categorization here is a combination/revision of earlier efforts by Bailyn (in *Ideological Origins*), Lundberg and May (in "Enlightened Reader in America"), and Greene (in *Intellectual Heritage*).

19. Max Farrand, ed., *The Records of the Federal Convention*, 4 vols. (New Haven, Conn: Yale University Press, 1966), 1:153–54, 164–65.

20. A more complete discussion of the findings is in Donald S. Lutz, "The Relative Influence of European Writers on Late Eighteenth Century American Political Thought," *American Political Science Review* 78 (March 1984): 189–97.

21. Ellis Sandoz is the most prominent theorist to address this neglected area in recent years. For entrée into the literature see *A Government of Laws: Political Theory, Religion, and the American Founding* (Baton Rouge: Louisiana State University Press, 1990). Sandoz also published a set of fifty-five sermons, which, when added to the sermons in the Hyneman and Lutz collection and to those in John Wingate Thornton's collection, include most of the sermons used in the citation study. See Ellis Sandoz, *Political Sermons of the American Founding Era, 1730–1805* (Indianapolis: Liberty Press, 1991); Charles S. Hyneman and Donald S. Lutz, *American Political Writing during the Founding Era, 1760–1805* (Indianapolis: Liberty Press, 1983); and John Wingate Thornton, *The Pulpit of the American Revolution* (Boston: Gould and Lincoln, 1860). See also Donald S. Lutz, *The Origins of American Constitutionalism* (Baton Rouge: Louisiana State University Press, 1988), chs. 2–4.

22. A useful discussion of the special status that these three men had at the constitutional convention can be found in Forrest McDonald, *Novus Ordo Seclorum: The Intellectual Origins of the Constitution* (Lawrence: University Press of Kansas, 1986), 209.

Chapter Six: Prolegomenon

1. Calvin C. Jillson, *Constitution Making: Conflict and Consensus in the Federal Convention of 1787* (New York: Agathon Press, 1988).

2. Christian Bay, *The Structure of Freedom* (Stanford, Calif.: Stanford University Press, 1970).

3. Martin Edelman, *Democratic Theories and the Constitution* (Albany: State University of New York Press, 1984).

4. For a sensible, straightforward entrée into the topic of political culture see Walter A. Rosenbaum, *Political Culture* (New York: Praeger, 1975).

5. Henry Tudor, *Political Myth* (New York: Praeger, 1972).

6. The characterization of Voegelin's theory is taken primarily from the introductions to Eric Voegelin, *Israel and Revelation* (Baton Rouge: Louisiana State University Press, 1956), and *The World of the Polis* (Baton Rouge: Louisiana State University Press, 1957), vols. 1 and 2 of *Order and History*. See also

Ellis Sandoz, ed., *Eric Voegelin's Significance for the Modern Mind* (Baton Rouge: Louisiana State University Press, 1991).

7. David Carr, *Time, Narrative, and History* (Bloomington: Indiana University Press, 1991), 163–64.

8. The distinction between logic-in-use and a reconstructed logic is taken from Abraham Kaplan, *The Conduct of Inquiry* (San Francisco: Chandler, 1964), especially pp. 3–11. The distinction continues to be a useful one, although what Kaplan makes of it is sometimes criticized. See Paul Diesing, *How Does Social Science Work? Reflections on Practice* (Pittsburgh: University of Pittsburgh Press, 1991).

Index

0 5 4 8